Mind
Your
Own
Business

Mind
Your
Own
Business

Whit Shaw

Tower Publishing Company
Portland, Maine

Printed in U.S.A.

Library of Congress catalog card number: 78-66096

ISBN: 0-89442-009-7

To my father, the best small businessman I've known, and to my wife, the most patient typist in the world.

Prologue

This book is an entrepreneurial venture in the true spirit of its title.

I have written expressly for the small business person frustrated by obstacles to success, but with the guts to persevere. MYOB is a basic how-to-do-it book that will show you:

How to start your own business—or buy one, or perhaps even inherit one, and

How to make the executive decisions that will keep your small business thriving and profitable and a joy to own forever.

Our libraries are full of volumes detailing the tasks, practices and responsibilities of managers of huge multinational corporations. I hope that one day you may graduate to these levels of expertise; remember that while 90 percent of all businesses today are small, 100 percent of them started out that way.

MYOB won't waste its pages (and your time) with expansive bibliographies, lists of small business investment companies or improbable venture capital sources. Such lists are dated and I hope this information isn't.

MYOB gives you the straight poop as I see it. The information, attitudes and practices outlined here have worked and continue to work for me and scores of my former students. If you apply them—and your-self—they will work for you. That will please me and make me a bit richer—and if that's not an entrepreneurial attitude, what is?

Author's Note

Much like squids, business writers protect themselves with clouds of impenetrable ink.

There are lots of bulky volumes stuffed with words that are of little help to the small businessman because they're obsolete before their pages dry.

Anyone seeking hard facts ready for application soon notices that most of these erudite chaps appear to be writing to impress each other.

That's not the case here, I think.

C.W.S.
Cape Elizabeth, Maine

Contents

And to My Only Son

Not very many of us have an uncle who struck it rich in the Australian opal mines, and even fewer have an uncle who S. I. R. and remembered us when he made out his will.

But there are lotsa people who inherit dear old dad's majority share of the plumbers' supply store.

Unfortunately, there are almost as many who want nothing to do with dad's bequest but spend the rest of their lives selling plumbers helpers and chrome faucets all week and moping around like Miniver Cheevy the rest of the time.

If someone leaves you a business or a piece of one, decide if you want to own and run it. Sure there will be family pressure. But you must use the same business sense you would in any other situation. Either plunge in and do your best or get out (sell) quickly; don't dilly-dally and allow others (or yourself) to run the business downhill.

Experience is an excellent school . . . but the tuition is very high, and most of its graduates are too old to work.

Whit Shaw

Grim Realities . . . What Are the Odds?

The first decision, of course, is whether to go on your own at all. Should you?

The possibilities for continued survival of a small private business appear to be slim indeed. Fewer than 50 percent make it through the first five years. The small businessman can lose it all—home, savings, self-confidence—when he can't cope.

Well, why try at all, then?

Let's examine the stats a little more closely . . . About half of the casualties are caused by *incompetence,* pure and simple negligence and total inattention to details of business.

If you remove this from consideration together with certain "easy entry" businesses such as bars, restaurants, food services and motels—and forget the entire farming picture—the statistics look much brighter.

If you avoid the just-listed pitfalls, you have already increased your chances of success to something over 70 percent. Better and better, right?

Sure, you know what you need to succeed; dedication, determination, knowledge of products, broad, well-rounded business experience, and of course bags and bags of money—anyone could tell you that and they'd be all wet.

Time is Prime

The major consideration in a small endeavor is *how you spend your productive time.*

Answer these questions truthfully about your projected business:

1. Does it match your life style?
2. Is it indoor or outdoor?
3. Will you deal with people or things?
4. Will they be your kind of people or your kind of things?
5. Will you be confined by the business or liberated by it?

Spend some time and think carefully—it's your life and your future you're pondering, and your family's as well.

The Choice

CASE NO. 1: Maxwell the car dealer runs a business grossing 2 million a year and earns a 35K salary.

CASE NO. 2: Sara, the unique product manufacturer, grosses $500,000 and pays herself twice Max's salary.

They are both small businesspersons; which is the more successful? Obviously, it's not the gross that counts, it's that *you do it yourself, for you.* Your strength, creativity and business enterprise reward you in direct proportion to your results.

Gone are the weekly paycheck, impressing the boss, paid vacations, security, the 40 hour week, retirement and all the rest of it.

Now you are on your own. And as I hope to show you, it can be worth it.

You're on your own!

Money alone sets all the world in motion.

Publilius Syrus, Maxim 656

When You're the Poor But Talented One

Brains, 60
Bucks, 40

Let's say you just came up with the business idea of the century—something really gigantic like another Polaroid. Something you've got the ability to see through to a handsome profit. But zounds! you are so flat the bank is about to repossess your cocker spaniel.

Find a partner who has cash and who desires to participate (because he recognizes your good idea). To him you suggest the following corporate structure:

Talent counts for 50 percent.

Cash funding counts for 50 percent.

So then you provide (in a $100,000 start-up example)

	out-of-pocket cost	percent of ownership
	----	50
100 percent of the talent		
20 percent of the funding	$20.000.	10
	$20,000.	60 percent

And your partner provides	----	0
None of the talent	$80,000.	40
80 percent of the funding		
		40 percent

And this is the way you go into your project
with minimal investment and majority
control. (If Warbucks won't play, find
another Warbucks; your ideas *are* worth
money!)

"Gentlemen, our troubles are over."

9

Support Your Local Consultant

Think of a management consultant as a harbor pilot. There you are, a great big important freighter—or a dashing destroyer if you must—and you've just arrived at a suitably snug harbor. But you've never been there before and don't know much about local passages, tides, shoals or currents and you're not all that nimble at close maneuvering.

But the harbor pilot is, so you hire him to get you safely tied up at the dock. His experience is invaluable.

It's the same with the local management consultant. You want him to find you money, or solve some other short-range problems; you don't plan to marry him.

Forget the "fat" firms

The only effective consultants for your purposes are the local solo practice types. The big institutional firms are terribly expensive and terribly ineffective for a small business in need of fine tuning—or major surgery, for that matter. A local consultant

11

(and there will be one, familiar with your area, no matter where you operate) will be quickly available and able to get his head into your problem. More important, he'll know local and regional conditions and can use this knowledge to solve your dilemma.

Chances are that your dilemma is the common one: you need money. Here's what a good consultant will do:

1. Determine the type of financing package and the amount needed.
2. Form a financing structure to meet that need.
3. Shape your analyses and proposals into a form suitable for potential investors, institutional or private.
4. Help select the best list of investors.
5. Present your plan for (or with) you.
6. Help you through the legal alder swamp with such necessities as letter of intent, buy/sell agreements, closing documents and so on. Chances are you will really need help here, so don't rely solely on your consultant. Get a lawyer or use your consultant's lawyer. (You bet he has one.)
7. Offer continuing assistance.

Point no. 3 above is more important than you think at first. Your banker will listen more attentively if you come in to see him dressed soberly (the way he is) and if your proposal is structured in a form familiar to him. Your consultant will have dealt with this banker and dozens of others like him,

and will have learned over the years to or-
chestrate presentations to emphasize
factors that will insure a "yes". He's had
sufficient feedback from bank officials to
know just what each is looking for.

Two last points:

Buying
advice

Finding sources of capital is a specialized
business in which experience is of significant help. So do what your man tells you
to, and back him all the way. He knows more
about his field than you do. That's why you
hired him, isn't it?

Ask about his fees or charges the very first
time you meet (to avoid misunderstanding
later, of course.) A good consultant makes a
lot of money, but if he can do for you what
you never could, he's worth it!

"*I'm a member of the business community.*"

Tycoonery and Its Blessings

Many millions of words of business prose have been written for the aid and comfort of those in high places, telling the tycoon how happy he is. But relative financial success and happy life style really are not reflections of the size of the endeavor.

Take the case of the proprietor of Frenchy's Chinese Hand Laundry and Aluminum Siding Company, who pays himself $20,000 a year. Now is the head of IBM, say, who earns some 20 or 30 times as much 20 or 30 times as happy? or fulfilled? *The small entrepreneur has a better chance of attaining personal goals.*

Escape the Urban Hassle

7

Remember the last time you vacationed in East Mitten, Vermont? Jeez, you thought, what a great place to live! I could fish and play tennis and the kids would know what grass (real grass) looks like and the wife wouldn't have to struggle with the goddamn traffic and my insurance rates would be lower and everything would be hotsy-totsy—if only I could make a living here!

Good news, friends: *small businesses work best in the hinterlands!*

Current choices of the easiest states in which to operate include among others, Maine, New Hampshire, Vermont, Arkansas, West Virginia, in the east, and Montana, New Mexico and Wyoming further west. These states are almost entirely rural in character and more scenic than a nude Joey Heatherton or whoever, revolving slowly on a pedestal, actively looking for small businesses too!

In more urban states, steer clear of the cities. The city environment is awfully harsh

Head for the hills!

for such a delicate little flower as your own small business—and in many cases deliberately so: no tax breaks (often penalties instead), restrictive codes, higher insurance rates of all types, unreliable labor force, higher wages, higher taxes, higher rents . . . you could continue the list as well as I.

Who wants the hassle? The possibility for nearly any life style is infinitely better in the boonies; so by all means consider the role of country folk.

And the living is easy

One last consideration; you can live better in a small town for any given salary than you can in the city.

Remember, of course, to check it out thoroughly and at first hand before you make the move. Talk with town officers, educators, local businessmen—whoever can tell you what you need to know.

There's no reason at all why you should ever regret your move.

The Business of Buying Your Own Business

First and most important is your determination and firm resolve to give up the cozy job and become the entrepreneur.

You should look at dozens of businesses before making up your mind. If nothing else, you will gain experience by the repeated exposure to many propositions. The classified ads will always say that the owner is selling because of poor health. More likely, it's the health of his business that is in a terminal situation.

You can consider running blind ads proclaiming your desires and screen those that respond. You'll soon meet an interesting gaggle of fellow business persons.

A more productive technique . . . contact major banks in the area, particularly those with large trust departments. Accounting firms are also sources to be considered. Avoid the temptation to become enthusiastic for only one particular business or type of business—play the field. Look at them all!

Most advertised businesses are doubtless overpriced and their owners are usually so inexperienced that even if you do get into negotiations, chances of closing the deal are slim. Through naïvete, the seller will feel that no concessions are in order, and it is unlikely that you will want to meet all of the seller's demands.

Consultant-Brokers

Consultant-Brokers will act in behalf of sellers and buyers and should be considered as the prime type of advisor. You'll find that they come in various breeds. They tend to be first class salesmen. Avoid the "finder" who hopes to get a fee just for telling you that Ed's restaurant is for sale and the real estate broker who calls himself a "commercial" real estate broker. "Commercial" real estate brokers are just fine if you're looking for apartment buildings, warehouses, Mom and Pop variety stores, vacant buildings, office space, etc.; but, if it's an operating, going business you want, the real estate types are of little help.

Consultant-Brokers frequently charge a retainer fee, ranging from several hundred to several thousand dollars; and also, charge a "commission" (from the seller) usually from 2% to 7% on a declining scale, depending upon size.

Before contacting a broker of any type, carefully outline what you have to offer. The more capable a manager you are and the more experience you bring to the new business, the less money you may need "up front" to buy it. If you are a neophyte in the prospective enterprise, expect to pay cash.

If you have a long track record at various levels of management and you know the industry and product well, there are ways to avoid the need for much of your own cash. As we've said elsewhere, cash is *NOT* the most important factor.

Once you know your own financial limitations, a knowledgeable consultant-broker can show you how to leverage, borrow, sell equity, and to an extent, how the business *CAN FINANCE ITSELF*.

The whole search is likely to take quite some time. It is coincidence if you do it in less than six months.

Before deciding among the dozen or so possibilities you turn up, ask yourself; does it meet your criteria, is it consistent with your plans, will the management which you are buying—or which you don't want, stay or leave, and how much will it cost you to have them stay or leave?

Take time, Dig deep

In contacting each prospective seller, firmly request his financial summaries, preferably for the past three to five years, even if the reports are only in rough form (or simply his tax returns). If you cannot interpret the financial statements—and relatively few buyers can—turn to an advisor for help.

Your consultant-broker or accountant will go over the statements and become as active as you want him to in determining the true assets of a business, its debts and credit strengths, inventories, receivables, plant and equipment.

At this point, the critical question is, what are you buying, what is the business? Many times what appears to be a manufacturing business is in truth a marketing business, or an assembly business, or a distribution business. Consider where you fit into the scheme of the business; what are you bringing to it; if the seller leaves the business, what is he taking out of it?

Professional advice is essential; but find yourself a consultant-broker who is running or has operated his own business. He may tell you only what experience he has had in the business. In the final analysis, you must be the expert who determines if the business fits you, and if you can contribute anything to its greater future success.

Projected cash flow, earnings, assets and the liabilities are obvious elements on the statements that require close examination. They are not, however, the greatest source of difficulty. Most acquisitive problems arise in two basic areas; the buyer does not understand the technology of the business and/or the business is undercapitalized and the seller has relied on borrowing money instead of making it.

I use a letter that I call "the initial agreement-in-principle." After buyer and seller sign it, this letter makes firming up of details for the final purchase-sale agreement much easier and usually insures greater success.

Traditionally, it is the buyer's broker or attorney who draws the agreement. The attorney, although he represents the buyer's legal interests, should look at the deal from both sides. A buyer's lawyer, for example, should consider the seller's problems and points of view.

From contract to closing

From contact to closing, the purchase procedure generally follows this path. After initial discussion between principals and the hand-shaking, agreement-in-principle is reached. A non-binding letter of intent or summary of terms is drawn which can be most helpful in smoking out some of the eventual problems. The sooner you face the problems, the better; and a good letter of intent avoids misunderstanding.

The letter of intent is followed by careful purchase investigation which leads to the purchase-sale agreement with exhibits and disclosures.

The buyer and seller are at opposite ends of the tug-of-war. The buyer wants indemnification, the seller wants to get out clean. Later you may want to take the seller to court over a huge inventory change, and if it isn't in your final agreement, tough!

The time between the signing of the purchase-sale agreement and the closing should be as short as possible, preferably simultaneous.

The closing should be just "a waltz around the conference table." Hopefully the work has all been done. I always prepare a little script (if the buyer's lawyer hasn't). It's a little like directing the school play . . . and they all live happily thereafter. . . .

Take Special Heed in These Areas

1. So called multiples or ratios are completely worthless to the buyer of a small business (i.e., you should pay 3.5 x annual earnings for a wholesale plumbing & heating business, etc). Use them for conversation with the seller (only if they favor your purpose).

2. A history of good earnings is a comforting indication, but really nothing much to hang your hat on and certainly nothing to pay money "up-front" for.

3. We have warned you previously that goodwill is a fleeting fiction. Never buy it, but if the seller is adamant and you must, at least call it something else on the buy-sell agreement, something you can depreciate. That's your privilege. Insist on it!

4. Poor past earnings mean little in a small, closely controlled business situation. There are a multitude of other, more important variables, most of them

25

contingent on the abilities of incoming management.

5. Remember, insist on re-casting all assets of your new business on the buy-sell agreement. It is your legal right to do this. (In the event your buy is an asset purchase.)

6. Above all, find the best and most experienced advice available. Take your time, apply the same logic and thoughtfulness that you exercise in your day to day business decisions. I have seen the havoc and resulting financial shambles wrought upon buyers of businesses by those "protecting their interests." Unfortunately, this often includes well intentioned but inexperienced attorneys and other professionals. Use a broker-consultant or attorney who has travelled this rocky road before. If in doubt, call me. It's too big a decision to bungle!

I've been rich and I've been poor . . . and let me tell you, honey, rich is better.

Sophie Tucker

If You Can't Trust Your Banker . . .

People deal with people, so look for a good banker, not a good bank.

Is your prospective banker knowledgeable? willing? does he have empathy with your endeavors? can the two of you communicate well together? is his attitude a positive one? lastly, does he *want* to help?

Something to remember: Whatever else you may do, choose a banker who can make a decision on the amount of money you want (don't be bashful—ask him his discretionary loan limit). There is absolutely no sense in going through your entire act in front of Fred Flunky, who can only repeat what he remembers of it at the next meeting of the loan committee.

No one—but no one—is more knowledgeable and convincing on the subject of your business than you, so before you waste everybody's time, be certain the banker has the authority to act.

Put yourself in your banker's shoes (sensible, black and well shined). He's in a highly regulated business, and up front he wants to know two main things:

1. Can your business handle the debt service obligation? (Can you pay it back?)
2. What collateral or other guarantee can the bank look to to secure its interest solidly? (How can the bank collect if you can't pay it back?)

Don't take a single turndown as final. One man's meat is another man's poison, so if banker no.1 says nay, modify your presentation to neutralize the reason for the refusal and proceed directly to the next banker.

Your presentation will be getting smoother with each effort. Never hesitate to admit that you have been turned down at another bank; simply imply that you are hopeful that he will exercise more objectivity and creativity (banking is such a dull business that bankers love to be thought creative, much as gamblers love to be thought respectable).

Lastly, thank God for our highly competitive banking system. If your proposal has real merit—and maybe if it hasn't—you will find a banker who agrees with you—and who backs his judgment with cash.

Money answereth all things.

Ecclesiastes

Money—It Doesn't Grow on Trees

Most business funds flow from—and through—our banking system. But there is a fundamental disadvantage to bank financing: it has to be paid back!

(The usual way, of course, is to repay interest and principal on a regular contractual basis, the standard installment note. The problem for you is that a new business may not produce an immediate profit and thus you can't afford the "debt service.")

Happily, there are other choices. First, a few definitions: *Venture Capitalists* are the folks who will give you money for a share in your enterprise, and *Equity Capital* is the term for the monies that they provide. In return for their dollars, you will have to give up "a piece of the action."

Equity: your pie, their dough

In order to take O.P.M. (other people's money) you should *structure yourself as a corporation.* That statement is a generalization, but such a course is usually a prudent one. (See the related chapters elsewhere in this book.)

The big advantage of equity financing is that there is no requirement that the monies be repaid! (At least not right away.)

If there is a secret to finding equity financing, it lies in the word "organization." Here is what you must do:

1. Write down a reasonable and concise summary of your business plan. Just what do you propose?
2. Draw up a *pro forma business statement* (a projection of how much money you think you can make). This pro forma should consist of:
   a. Your *objectives,* simply stated.
   b. A *balance sheet** at start-up and after one and two years.
   c. An *operating or earnings statement** projected for at least two years.
   d. A *cash flow projection** for the two-year period.
3. Structure this summary for the particular person or group. You *must* know what those considering your proposal are looking for and give them every opportunity to say yes.

*Refer to section on Financial Statements for basic samples of these.

Sometimes It Grows on Trees

Okay. You have your idea and a sample of your product and you're ready to draw up a keen and concise operating statement as just discussed. But who do you draw it up *for*? Who do you approach for money?

As the saying goes, "The woods are full of them." Here's a list of those wonderful folks who will press their money on you, starting close to home:

1. Your family. In most cases, we can assume that those nearest and dearest will support you in your endeavors as much as they can. But *tread lightly.* The very fact of your closeness will be the cause of great trauma if your business is not a smashing success; and you can't just walk away from a damaged social relationship. Emphasize the great degree of risk and then think seriously about *not* taking money from members of your family.

2. Social friends. Obviously the same caveats apply as above, but to a lesser degree. Perhaps you'd best use friends as social contacts to develop other prospects.
3. Suppliers/clients/business associates. Your doctor, lawyer, professional and commercial acquaintances; all excellent sources.
4. I hold that the best source of all is once removed from the above; a colleague of your doctor friend, for example. Incidentally, I have found that among the professional and educated ranks generally, *the more education, the less business sophistication.* Most such people have never been trained to evaluate a business proposition and accordingly will be inclined to accept your expertise at face value.

   It is helpful if you are recommended to these prospects. In that way they learn only good and productive things about you and your proposition. They don't hear that you beat your wife, eat your peas with a knife, and have gone through three business failures in four years. Such a positive approach is entirely to your benefit, and you can close a deal with such people rather easily.
5. Make a "limited offer" within the boundaries of your state. Prepare a little pamphlet with an introduction and a pro forma business statement, and brace yourself for some red tape (to comply

with your state banking commission's regs.)

6. Visit your "local venture capital corporation." A federally financed (SBIC) will help, either with a loan or by backing a commercial loan, but you will find that it is of considerable help to be black, red, underprivileged, culturally deprived, handicapped or what have you. If these conditions of extremis don't apply in your case, try private venture capital. You'll find a higher degree of sophistication. Your ideas and proposal *must be sound* and your projections documented and valid.

7. Go to a venture capital finder. Such an organization will put you on a computerized list and distribute it among thousands of people who have signified their willingness to invest. You will pay a fee, say $200 to $500 up front and you will not get this money back, even if you don't get funding.

8. Consider a "private offering" in two or three states. This will require planning, professional assistance and extra expense, and you must conform to all the state regulations involved. It ain't easy.

9. Going public. A public stock offering is a complex undertaking and will involve a relationship with underwriters and jillions of other people and things. You probably shouldn't pursue this course.

10. Private monies looking for a place to hide. Sometimes a businessman may be looking for a legitimate spot in which to

invest some money, say for a tax advantage. Your proposal may fill his requirements as neatly as his cash fills yours.

Reminder: *Whatever you do, always structure your plan carefully for tax advantage—your tax advantage.*

Always, always, always: State and document the high risk factors to all of your investors (but wait until they are thoroughly sold on the project). A specific disclosure letter is an excellent way to do this; ask your attorney.

Never, under any circumstances, take any funds that a person *cannot really afford* to give to you.

Sure there are other sources of money:
Small loan companies. Higher interest rates.
Insurance loans. Lower rates.
Real Estate Investment Trusts.
Credit cards. Up to $10,000 if you're a good enough risk.
Personal loans by mail. But if the people who know you won't loan you money . . .
You can always overuse your local credit, but that is certainly a last resort.
You could even get pumped up by signing a personal note from a second mortgage specialist, bank, or savings and loan institution.

The list could continue, but as it does, the more complicated the deals become, and the higher the level of sophistication you need.

Let's end with the gentle hint that if you have exhausted all the conventional sources and still haven't found a "yes," perhaps you should rethink your whole project. *Maybe all those people are telling you something.*

Three for a Quarter

Somewhere along the road to becoming an entrepreneur you will have to price your product.

The traditional way is to base your charge on your cost (labor, material, overhead, and marketing cost) plus a reasonable markup. *This method is all wet.* Forget it if you can; the resulting price is always too low. If you are using this system, you are not getting enough for your product.

Some businessmen base their price on competition and/or tradition. That's wrong, too. They have so little confidence in their own product that one wonders why they're in business.

Sure, many factors must be considered in your decision. To begin with, the laws of supply and demand, and the interplay of natural forces; and also sealed bids, negotiated prices, obsolescence, quantity discounts, seasonal discounts, new products, economic conditions, political unrest, geographical distribution problems, lease/buy alternatives, shortages, tax increases, about fifty other factors that apply especially to your product or service, and at least as many more that apply uniquely to *you.* Consider all of them.

Be aware—painfully aware—that inflation and increased costs are your constant business companions!

You must have absolute confidence in the superiority of your goods or services: the biggest single factor in setting your prices is where you value them.

You must ask for the maximum price you can get. And that's the only rule you need to know.

I used to think that money was the most important thing in life. Now that I am old, I know it is.

Oscar Wilde

Under the Spreading Tax-Free Tree . . .

You don't have to incorporate, of course, but you probably should, and here are some powerful reasons why, all related to taxes:

1. The corporate form may be used as a tax shelter.
2. Corporations in foreign trade or in other ventures can get special exemptions.
3. Members of a family may be stock-holders without many of the burdens and restrictions of family partnerships.
4. The corporate form makes it possible for owner/executives to realize better wealth-building advantages under a corporate pension or profit-sharing plan.
5. Death benefits up to $5,000 can be paid tax-free to beneficiaries of a stock-holder-employee.
6. By incorporating you avoid questions of your right to deduct losses. Individuals can deduct losses in full only if incurred in a trade or business or in transactions

entered into for profit, or losses. Corporations are not so restricted. All losses are assumed to be incident to the business of the corporation.

7. Deferred compensation and stock retirement plans can be used to achieve the financial planning purposes of the owner, his family and employees.

8. Only 15 percent of dividend income is taxed to the corporation; 100 percent to the partnership.

9. The corporate form may facilitate saving income and estate taxes by gifts to children or a family foundation.

10. A new corporation or partnership is a new taxpayer. There may be a substantial advantage in electing new tax options.

11. A corporation may be able to carry insurance on the lives of owner/executives at a reduced annual tax cost and then, without any further income tax burden, realize the proceeds and make them available to pay estate taxes. Working stockholders are eligible for $50,000 of tax-free group insurance coverage.

12. Reopening of the partners' tax years is possible with IRS examination of partnerships. This is a serious disadvantage in a partnership.

13. Corporation stockholders can often control the dividend processes. Therefore, unlike partners, they usually can dictate the year they get income. They might often select the most favorable

year. Control of dividends by corporate holders permits averaging of income over a long period.

14. Stockholders have a capital gain when the corporation is liquidated. This is not always so with a partnership. Stockholders may be able to liquidate in a year when they have losses to offset the gain from the liquidation.

15. Corporations may get an immediate refund if they sustain a net operating loss. They may reduce the tax still due (if any) for the prior year, if they have losses in the current year. Partners must wait a year to get the same treatment, since they pay as they go.

16. A special provision protects the tax-free withdrawal of accumulated corporate profits in an amount equal to death taxes and expenses on death of an owner/stockholder through a partial stock redemption.

17. A corporation is allowed to accumulate earnings, free from penalty, for purposes of redeeming stock to pay death taxes of one or more of the owners.

18. A corporation is also allowed, under certain circumstances, to accumulate earnings to redeem the stock held by a private foundation.

19. The owners are not likely to be hit for ordinary income when their interest is sold and the business has substantially appreciated inventory. Presence of such property in a partnership gives rise to full tax on the appreciation if a partner

sells his interest or if he dies or retires.
20. The working owners get the benefit of tax-free medical and hospital insurance, and the corporation is entitled to deduct its cost.
21. The working owners also get tax-free treatment for salary continuation payments made on account of sickness or accident.
22. Another incidental benefit concerns meals and lodging. Working stockholders may exclude from income the value of any meals or lodging furnished by the corporation for its convenience.

Whew! (Now do you see?)

Elsewhere in this little tome you will find a list of tax advantages of incorporation. As you might suspect, there are disadvantages also. Not nearly so many, to be sure, but to be fair, let's give them equal time:

1. Cost. Depending on the state you live in and the lawyer you select, the price of incorporating will be between $50 and $1,000.
2. Red Tape. There are vast amounts of paperwork required by governmental agencies. Remember, you are creating a new entity with all the resulting consequences!

Small business requires management of a high order. First and foremost it needs strategy!

Peter F. Drucker

Plan Ahead

Call it a game plan, sales forecast, or what-ever. Today more and more small owners/managers look to long-range strategies to insure success. So must you.

We live in a world where the only certainty is change. And at an accelerating rate, at that.

One significant fact stands out: No longer is any market confined to a single town, county, state, or region. We are fast becoming a one-world marketplace. You have more influence than you think.

The reverse is true also, and it's a pity. Far-off people and things affect you. The Arab oil embargo of late 1973 focused world attention on the disagreeable fact of a growing energy shortfall. This squeeze—and it is just beginning—has resulted in (1) higher prices for energy and (2) uncertain and/or diminishing supply. When you couple these factors with rising costs of raw materials and a restive labor pool, you've got trouble with a capital T.

While we're at it, let's list some other factors that will affect you, whether you want them to or not:

Government controls: Cleaning up your smokestack or wastewater discharge will decrease your profitability; but you have a moral and legal obligation to do it, and pronto. Controls are everywhere and they will expand.
Inflation: It's been almost impossible for companies big or small to cope with inflationary pressures (because it is impossible to measure the future with precision. If GM can't do it, can you?).
Tariff and trade barriers: If you've bought any inexpensive shirts or shoes lately, have you noticed where they were made? Imports do affect *you.*

The only way a little, unprotected fish like you has a chance in this great big ocean is to out-think the big fish, or to taste so bad or be so agile they won't swallow you. FoMoCo is not interested in buying out Zeke's Bicycle Shop and Toaster Repair Company.

But Z's B. S. and T. R. Co. is affected by inflation and energy costs and so on, and it needs a game plan as badly as Ford does.

Here's how Zeke goes about setting one up:

1. Develop general objectives and sales goals.
2. Appraise your company's strengths and weaknesses realistically.
3. Set specific goals.

4. Draw up market strategies. Plan your tactics artfully.
5. Keep your plan flexible and simple.
6. Reduce it to written form.
7. Use, revise it, refer to it—and do all these on a continuing basis.

It is easy—and deadly—to say, "yeah, sure," and keep some objectives in the back of your head where you can sift through them in spare moments. What you need is *discipline.* Write your marketing strategies down, and refer to them on schedule. Rethink them the first Monday of every month—every Monday if need be.

Your plan should be a living, growing entity. There are so many things you can't influence that you have to work hard on the things you can.

No one ever said it would be easy.

The Business Plan Resume

A resume must be included with your business plan which you take to your banker, venture capital source, or whoever you expect to borrow from.

Probably you already have a resume stuffed away from your last job expedition, and that's half the battle; but you must modify it. You must impress your money source with your competence and managerial experience; show what you *can do* as well as what you *have done. The resulting document may also be valuable when soliciting future clients.*

And here's how to do it:

1. Name, home address and phone, business address and phone.
2. Personal data, marital status, etc.
3. Education, last grade first.
4. Business background and experience, most recent first.
5. Special interests, abilities, hobbies (if they would help).
6. References.

Sections 3, 4 and 5 are the biggies, so concentrate. You can't do much about your education, although if you were valedictorian, on the honors list consistently, or whatever, you should certainly mention it.

As regards business experience, don't just say:

> July 1978—August 1980: Fry cook at Sam's Clams, Starting salary $100/wk; final salary $170/wk.

How much better to put it *all* down, and say it like this:

> July 1978—August 1980: Chef at Sam's Clams. Assumed responsibility for enlarging menu and rearranging seating with consequent 85 percent increase in gross sales and 105 percent in net. Redesigned kitchen—without interrupting service—to effect smoother work flow. Supervised enlargement of parking lot and general outside landscaping.

Cooking short orders in a clam shack may not be the way to a million, but if you were holding the purse strings, which of the above paragraphs would grab you?

Got a hobby? It can help.

The same tenets apply for the special interests section. If you coach a Little League baseball team, of course you should put it in; it shows that you have managerial talents and experience. Are you (or have you been) an officer in the local PTA? Put that in. In the community Little Theatre group? Include it. (On the other hand, if your only outside interest is your collection of exotic prewar French postcards, best keep it to yourself . . . your banker might not understand.)

Once again, the burden of my theme is, *make it easy for your money source to say yes.*

Financial Statements

So. You've just invented a new whatso, miles ahead of anything else on the market, and you have succeeded in putting together a nice little company to cover the country waist-deep in Willy's Retrograde Whatsos.

You have financing, two alert employees, and a nice old barn to work in. Good for you! Now you can settle down and devote your time and energies to R and D, right?

Wrong! You will have to develop *accounting skills* (if you don't already have them), and the sooner the better. Accounting, like its cousin, math, has received a bad press in this country; many people don't like it, don't understand it, and wish it would go away. But skill in finance is at least as important as skill in selling, or production, or any other of the elements that make up today's complex business arena.

If you are running a steam locomotive, you depend on the gauges and dials to tell you what the pressure inside the boiler is, how much fuel you have left, and everything else you need to know. It is not enough to feel the outside of the boiler jacket, decide it's warm enough, and go charging down the track. After all, this is the Twentieth Century.

Well, your income statements and balance sheets are your gauges and dials. They are there all the time, registering internal conditions, and you had better learn how to read them.

I can hear your response: "Don't talk to me, I can't bother with the technical stuff." You certainly can leave the details to the pros, but you must understand and relate to this important documentation of your efforts.

The following are just a few simple examples of the form that the principal financial records take.

1. Operating or income start-up.
2. Balance sheet (your assets—liabilities) or statement of net worth.
3. Cash flow statement.

Don't look so distressed. If other people can do it, you can do it. Let's take one step at a time . . .

THE OLD SODA POP SHOP

Projected Balance Sheet
Current Status (after purchase of business) vs. One Year Later
(in even hundreds)

	Start up Date	one year later
ASSETS		
Current Assets		
Cash on Hand and in Bank	$ 5,000	$ 30,000
Accounts Receivable	0	2,000
Inventory	30,000	31,000
Total Current Assets	35,000	63,000
Fixed Assets		
Pick-up Truck	5,000	5,000
Ice Machine	1,000	1,000
Coolers	1,000	1,000
Delicatessen Case	700	700
Appliances & Fixtures	500	500
Total	8,200	8,200
Less Allowance for Depreciation	0	(2,000)
Net Fixed Assets	8,200	6,200
Other Assets		
License	2,000	2,000
Leasehold improvements	5,000	5,000
Total Other Assets	7,000	7,000
TOTAL ASSETS	50,200	76,200
LIABILITIES		
Current Liabilities		
Accounts Payable	0	12,000
Federal Income Tax Withheld	0	300
Federal S. S. Tax Payable	0	200
Sales Tax Payable	0	1,000
Principal Payments Due, Long-Term Loan	5,000	5,000
Total Current Liabilities	5,000	18,500
Long-Term Loan	25,000	20,000
TOTAL LIABILITIES	30,000	38,500
NET WORTH	20,200	37,700
Total Liabilities Plus Net Worth	50,200	76,200

Operating Statement for the Years 1976, 1977, 1978
with Pro Forma Statement for 1979 (Unaudited)

PEDAL PUSHERS, INC.

	1978	1979	1980	1981
Gross Sales	3,649.15	29,712.18	56,401.30	70,000.
Less: Cost of Goods Sold				
Inventory Jan. 1 of year		1,882.83	4,777.99	---
Purchases	4,099.04	25,831.12	27,010.97	---
Freight In	134.10	733.65	865.75	---
Goods available for sale	4,233.14	28,447.60	32,654.71	---
Inventory Dec. 31 of year	1,882.83	4,777.99	6,594.00	
Merchandise dating order 5-10-78			3,106.75	
TOTAL			9,700.75	
Total Cost of Goods Sold	2,350.31	23,669.61	32,953.96	39,500.
Gross Profit on Sales	1,298.84	6,042.57	23,447.34	30,500.
Less: Operating Expenses				
Rent	879.00	1,825.00	2,177.49	2,200.
Advertising	67.19	1,385.26	726.86	1,000.
Telephone & Electricity	307.01	1,037.93	1,344.81	1,400.
Personal Property Taxes		195.86	207.19	225.
Insurance	209.00	208.00	252.46	275.
Office Expense & Postage	220.03	348.58	268.66	300.
Shop Supplies & Expense	163.60	424.49	740.71	750.
Dues & Subscriptions		92.40		
Repairs		154.86	114.07	150.
Depreciation	17.06	56.64	128.93	200.
Professional Fees		25.00	255.00	500.
Payroll			1,272.50	2,600.
Payroll Taxes			74.44	150.
Total Operating Expense	1,862.89	5,754.02	7,563.12	9,750.
NET OPERATING PROFIT (loss)	(564.95)	288.55	15,884.22	20,750.

Pro Forma Operating Statement for

DUDLY DRUG COMPANY

(even thousands)

	1st Year	2nd Year
Gross Sales	$150,000.	$190,000.
Less cost of Sales (54%)	81,000.	102,000.
Gross Profit	69,000.	88,000.
Variable/Fixed Expense		
Salaries	18,000	24,000
Rent (net)	6,000	1,000
Insurance & Taxes	1,500	1,500
Caswell-Massey fees	2,000	2,000
Telephone & utilities	1,000	1,000
Bank Interest	1,200	1,100
Advertising	3,000	3,000
Legal & Accounting	2,000	1,000
Office Supplies	2,000	1,200
Taxes & Misc.	500	500
Total Expenses	$37,200	$36,300
Net Profit or (loss) before depreciation, F.I.T. or owners' compensation	31,800	51,700

Note: Rent 2nd year is net considering participation of pharmacy area.

DUDLY DRUG COMPANY

Projected Cash Flow for Six Months
(in even hundreds)

	1st	2nd	3rd	4th	5th	6th
Opening Cash Balance (cash on hand 1st day)	$20,000.	$ 4,300.	$15,000.	$19,000.	$24,000.	$29,000.
Plus						
Bank loan receipts	5,000.	10,000.	--	--	--	--
Pharmacy lease	200.	300.	300.	500.	500.	500.
Cash in from sales	1,000.	6,500.	12,000.	15,000.	15,000.	15,000.
Total cash available	$26,200.	$21,100.	$27,300.	$34,500.	$39,500.	$44,500.
Less						
Cost of inventory	12,000.	3,000.	6,000.	8,000.	8,000.	8,000.
Fixtures & leasehold improvements	5,000.	--	--	--	--	--
Caswell-Massey fees	2,000.	--	--	--	--	--
Rent & telephone	1,000.	500.	500.	500.	500.	500.
Insurance & taxes	--	100.	100.	100.	100.	100.
Bank payment	--	--	200.	200.	200.	200.
Advertising	200.	500.	300.	300.	300.	300.
Legal & accounting	700.	500.	100.	100.	100.	100.
Salaries	1,000.	1,000.	1,000.	1,000.	1,000.	2,000.
Office supplies	--	500.	100.	100.	100.	100.
Cash Out this Month	$21,900.	6,100.	8,300.	10,300.	10,300.	11,300.
Ending Cash	4,300.	15,000	19,000.	24,200.	29,200.	33,200.

*Notes to cash flow—next page

DUDLY DRUG COMPANY

Proposed Financial Package
(Funds to be expended / or committed prior to opening)

USE OF FUNDS	SOURCE OF FUNDS		
	Loan	*Equity*	*Total*
Start-Up			
Caswell-Massey fee		2,000.	2,000
Legal & Accounting etc.		1,500	1,500
Advertising		1,000	1,000
Inventory	15,000		15,000
Fixture & leasehold improvements		5,000	5,000
Other			
Office supplies	500		500
Rent deposit (2 mos)	1,000		1,000
Insurance—deposits	500		500
Total			$26,500

SWAMP CITY TRACTOR & EQUIPMENT COMPANY

Operating Statement
(in even thousands)
(you use exact figures)

	Current Year
Sales	$270,000
Cost of Sales	
Inventory—beginning	120,000
Purchases	150,000
	270,000
Inventory—ending	100,000
	170,000
Gross Profit	$100,000
Expenses	
Wages	35,000
Advertising	2,000
Travel expense	2,000
Shop supplies	1,000
Radio—telephone	1,000
Office expense	3,000
Repairs	1,000
Light, heat & power	5,000
Insurance	6,000
Taxes	3,000
Depreciation	1,000
Legal & Accounting	2,000
Total	$ 62,000
Debt Service Expense (interest)	10,000
TOTAL EXPENSES	. 72,000
NET INCOME	$ 28,000

Accounting for Those Who Hate Accounting

It is unfortunate but true, that you will find 85 percent of all the highest level accounting (and, it follows, accountants) hopelessly tied to tax avoidance. Tax evasion is another matter entirely, and if diligently pursued will get you room and board at Uncle Sam's Hard Rock Hilton.

But what about the poor small business-man who hasn't made enough money yet even to have a tax avoidance problem? It's an interesting question: first you have to *make money,* then you have to worry about *keeping it* legally (by not overpaying your taxes).

And the IRS says most small businesses do overpay their taxes.

O.K. How can an accountant be helpful to you? What services should you ask for? What should you expect to get?

Like the old recipe for a successful rabbit stew that starts, "First catch the rabbit," find an accountant. Sure you want a good one, so choose carefully. Look at the chapters on lawyers and consultants, and follow the same guidelines.

If your CPA has mouse breath

Why should you care if your accountant has bad breath, or is bald? You will never be closer than across the desk, so pick him for his brain. Let him sell himself to you rather than the other way around. You don't want an indifferent accountant.

What you're after is good advice and a sound system. In the first place, in-house accounting beats farmed-out (outhouse!) accounting by a country mile. Do all you can yourself, provided that *it is in a proper form.*

If you start with a simple system—and when you start your business is small and simple, isn't it?—the light will dawn and you will find you have an honest-to-Gawd tool that will help you.

You will know where you are and where you are going. And then you can spend your really productive time on the business of getting there faster.

Words You'll Hear Your Accountant Say

A Glossary

Acid Test Ratio—Cash plus those other assets which can be immediately converted to cash should equal, or exceed, current liabilities. The formula used to determine the ratio is as follows:

$$\frac{Cash\ +\ Receivables\ (net)\ +\ Marketable\ Securities}{Current\ Liabilities}$$

The "acid test" ratio is one of the most important credit barometers used by lending institutions, as it indicates the ability of a business enterprise to meet its current obligations.

Aging Receivables—A scheduling of accounts receivable according to the length of time they have been outstanding. This shows which accounts are not being paid in a timely manner and may reveal any difficulty in collecting long-overdue receivables. This may also be an important indicator of developing cash flow problems.

Amortization—To liquidate on an installment basis; the process of gradually paying off a liability over a period of time, i.e., a mortgage is amortized by periodically paying off part of the face amount of the mortgage.

Assets—The valuable resources, or properties and property rights owned by an individual or business enterprise.

Balance Sheet—An itemized statement which lists the total assets and the total liabilities of a given business to portray its net worth at a given moment in time.

Break-even Analysis—A method used to determine the point at which the business will neither make a profit nor incur a loss. That point is expressed in either the total dollars of revenue exactly offset by total expenses (fixed and variable); or in total units of production, the cost of which exactly equals the income derived by their sale.

Capital Equipment—Equipment which you use to manufacture a product, provide a service, or use to sell, store, and deliver merchandise. Such equipment will not be sold in the normal course of business, but will be used and worn out or be consumed as you do business.

Cash Flow—The actual movement of cash within a business: cash inflow minus cash outflow. A term used to designate the reported net income of a corporation plus amounts charged off for depreciation, depletion, amortization, and extraordinary charges to reserves, which are bookkeeping deductions and not actually paid out in cash. Used to offer a better indication of the ability of a firm to meet its own obligations and to pay dividends than with the conventional net income figure.

Cash Position—See Liquidity.

Corporation—An artificial legal entity created by government grant and endowed with certain powers; a voluntary organization of persons, either actual individuals or legal entities, legally bound together to form a business enterprise.

Current Assets—Cash or other items that will normally be turned into cash within one year, and assets that willl be used up in the operations of a firm within one year.

Current Liabilities—Amounts owed that will ordinarily be paid by a firm within one year. Such items include accounts payable, wages payable, taxes payable, the current portion of a long-term debt, and interest and dividends payable.

Current Ratio—A ratio of a firm's current assets to its current liabilities. The current ratio includes the value of inventories which have not yet been sold, so it is not the best evaluation of the current status of the firm. The "acid test" ratio, covering the most liquid of current assets, provides a better evaluation.

Deal—A proposal for financing business creation or expansion; a series of transactions and preparation of documents in order to obtain funds for business expansion or creation.

Depreciation—A reduction in the value of fixed assets. The most important causes of depreciation are wear and tear, the effect of the elements, and gradual obsolescence which makes it unprofitable to continue using some assets until they have been exhausted. The purpose of the *bookkeeping charge for depreciation* is to write off the original cost of an asset (less expected salvage value) by equitably distributing charges against operations over its entire useful life.

Entrepreneur—An innovator of a business enterprise who recognizes opportunities to introduce a new product, a new productive process, or an improved organization, and who raises the necessary money, assembles the factors of production and organizes an operation to exploit the opportunity.

Equity—The monetary value of a property or business which exceeds the claims and/or liens against it by others.

Illiquid—See Liquidity.

Liquidity—A term used to describe the solvency of a business, and which has special reference to the degree of readiness in which assets can be converted into cash without a loss. Also called Cash Position. If a firm's current assets cannot be converted into cash to meet current liabilities, the firm is said to be Illiquid.

Long-term Liabilities—These are liabilities (expenses) which will not mature within the next year.

Market—The number of people and their total spending (actual or potential) for your product line within the geographic limits of your distribution ability. The Market Share is the percentage of your sales compared to the sales of your competitors in total for a particular product line.

Net Worth—The owner's equity in a given business represented by the excess of the total assets over the total liabilities (the total amounts owed to outside creditors) at a given moment of time. Also, the net worth of an individual as determined by deducting the amount of all personal liabilities from the total value of personal assets.

Partnership—A legal relationship created by the voluntary association of two or more persons to carry on as co-owners of a business for profit; a type of business organization in which two or more persons agree on the amount of their contributions (capital and effort) and on the distribution of profits, if any.

Pro Forma—A projection or estimate of what may result in the future from actions in the present. A pro forma financial statement is one that shows how the actual operations of the business will turn out if certain assumptions are realized. The pro forma is informally known in the trade as a S.W.A.G. (Scientific Wild-Assed Guess).

Profit—The excess of the selling price over all costs and expenses incurred in making the sale. Also, the reward to the entrepreneur for the risks assumed in the establishment, operation and management of a given enterprise or undertaking.

Sole Proprietorship or Proprietorship—A type of business organization in which one individual owns the business. Legally, the owner *is* the business and personal assets are typically exposed to liabilities of the business.

Sub-Chapter S Corporation or Tax Option Corporation—A corporation which has elected under Sub-Chapter S (by unanimous consent of its shareholders) not to pay any corporate tax on its income and, instead, to have the shareholders pay taxes on it, even though it is not distributed. Shareholders of a tax option corporation are also entitled to deduct, on the individual returns, their shares of any net operating loss sustained by the corporation, subject to limitations in the tax code.

Takeover—The acquisition of one company by another company.

Target Market—The *specific* individuals, distinguished by socio-economic,

demographic, and/or interest characteristics, who are the most likely potential
customers for the goods and/or services of
a business.

Working Capital, Net—The excess of current
assets over current liabilities. These excess
current assets are available for carrying on
business operations.

The Bobbsey Twin Fallacy

I am irrevocably opposed to 50/50 corporations—ones in which ownership is
shared equally. Either stockholder can
disrupt the orderly flow of business at a
whim. If your old Pard Joe is served a break-
fast of burnt toast and overcooked egg, he
may well pull in the opposite direction all
day; if it's s-x problems at home or anywhere
else—he may well wreck the company;
bigger firms than yours have fallen for less.

One of the classic dilemmas, leaving
behind such dramatics as mentioned above,
is the situation of two little guys whose
business has enjoyed some success . . .
then one wants to expand and the other to
sell the business, take the money and run.
Sound advice: If you have committed cash
and effort, get 52% of the voting shares. If
you feel you must go the buddy/buddy
route, at least make sure to set up a buy-
in/buy-out agreement that can be executed
any time down the road.

Tipping
the scales

A case in point: Two young businessmen, former frat brothers at a New England college, formed a corporation for a new and exciting project. They selected a lawyer who said he would save them money and represent them both (!), who set up the corporate structure so that each owned half. Of course Black Monday arrived, disenchantment set in and the ensuing hassle scuttled the enterprise. (But the original idea was still good . . . it just didn't have a chance.)

It's fashionable to knock the institution of marriage these days. Deserving of these lumps or not, the prognosis for marriage is measurably better than for a 50/50 corporation. Someone has to be boss!

You heard it here first.

On Being Alone

We have spoken much of the solitary, self reliance of the entrepreneur - to enjoy being alone you have to enjoy the company you're keeping - like *yourself!* (ummm!)

You must be able to live contentedly and confidently within yourself, viewing the world around you with pragmatic optimism. On being an optimist Goethe said - "If you have hopes, tell me about them - if you have doubts, keep them to yourself, I already have enough of my own!"

If you are reduced to recidivist beggary in order to "be liked", (1) you may really be unhappy with yourself, (2) you must be surrounded with people - you "need people" and people who "need" people are not the luckiest people in the world, probably (3) you "overkill" - talk too long on the phone - are the last to leave a party - offer unrequested (and usually unwanted) personal advice.

Detach yourself now from cliches and popular images of what you *should* be. If you are not happy with (and by) yourself, all of the other moves that I suggest to bring you to the successful heights of entre- preneurism will be about as helpful as re- arranging the deck chairs on the Titanic.

Belly Right Up to the Bar

It is simply a shame that lawyers generally don't advertise their specialties. However, there's an encouraging recent trend toward advertising, *and* there's a healthy minority doing just that! Some of them love the world of business and can be concerned and helpful in your efforts to do well.

But beware! Most are no help at all. (And why should they be? They make more money escorting squabblers through the divorce courts or lovingly guiding massive estates through probate.) There are lawyers who chase ambulances, really. There are lawyers who limit their practices to the assistance of businesses in *exigeant termini,* otherwise known as deep s---. There are lawyers you wouldn't believe.

You should pick your lawyer with as much intelligent care as you pick your spouse, and for most of the same reasons. You're going to be together for a long time, through thick and lean, and you need someone by your side who will really cleave to you when the path is all uphill and thorny.

So level with your attorney / candidate in front. Does he like your business? Will he abandon his July 4 barbecue at home to come help you out? Is he on the make? (Cassius would have made a great lawyer.)

Look for one on the make

Hint: Shop about for a young one who is getting started with a good firm or just beginning in single practice. Having a good business attorney is like the systematic continuing program of preventive medicine that your doctor keeps harping about, except now we're discussing your business, not your bod.

Summary: Use your noggin. Hell, you can always find a good tennis partner . . .

Busy, Busy, Busy

There you are, slaving from dawn to dusk, working your trousers to the bone—just not enough hours in the day. Acting out such cliches is fine if you're working for some other guy. But when you're working for Old Number One, the new word for today is *productivity.*

What are the time-wasters?

At the top of the list is *meetings.* Any small business which has regularly scheduled meetings simply can't call itself productive. Seasoned small businessmen cite the meeting as the biggest time waster of all. They simply aren't effective for (1) making important decisions, (2) announcements of policy and (3) certainly not for getting expert advice. Such things are best accomplished on a one-to-one basis.

If you have a meeting, keep it short and have a (meaning one only) specific purpose in mind. The regular Monday morning meeting is an anachronism and it's high time you got the word.

Writing letters is another of my pet peeves—even if you know how to do it and you probably don't. The same business can be effectively operated by a person who writes three letters a week or by some dummy who relentlessly grinds out ten or twenty letters a day. How does the former do it?

Simple. Don't write all those letters. They take your time, the time of secretaries and the time of others who feel obliged to read them.

Give Ma Bell the business

Use the phone instead. (See section on Ma Bell.) It's cheaper, faster, more effective and more personal.

If you feel you must write a letter (to document something):

1. Express only one thought or idea in each letter.
2. Never write a letter longer than three paragraphs. Always keep it to one page.
3. Always end it by requesting action or asking agreement.

Now maybe—just maybe—your deathless words will receive the attention they deserve!

Another time-waster is *misapplied concentration.* You have a finite amount of brain-power and time, so apply them where they will do the most good. Concentrate on the sectors that are profitable, and phase out all that is not giving you proper value for effort spent.

Establishing goals and priorities is commendable, but between you and me, managing by "objective" is a childlike dream in today's harsh business jungle. It takes strategy to achieve these objectives to lift you above and beyond the masses of your unwashed competitors. Anything else is mental masturbation (which is to say that it feels good but it doesn't get you any for-warder).

Many small business operators have a *ritual of visitation* that involves their bank and post office. I wish someone would tell me why your friendly banker must be visited daily. Bank by mail (they pay the postage). Use night depositories. Reserve your calls on the banker to those required to obtain more capital and don't forget to wear your pinstripe suit (the one with the vest).

The post office is one of the few businesses that will deliver to your door (well, usually). 'Nuff said.

"*To my mind, the secret of executive performance is the ability to delegate authority. For instance, <u>nothing</u> ever reaches this desk.*"

Decisions

De minimis non curat praetor (the magistrate does not consider trifles).

That is Roman law from two thousand years ago . . . Heed it! Don't bog yourself down by considering the little things that don't influence the end result.

The effective decision-maker also compares the risk and effort involved in action to the risk involved in doing nothing at all! Many of the things the business operator worries about never happen anyway.

Do the best you can and then *don't worry.*

The size of the problems that concern a businessperson reflect the size of that person's business capabilities.

Seest thou a man diligent in his business? He shall stand before kings.

Proverbs

Gently Rapping at Your Door

Every change in the economy, every new government action, *creates new opportunities* for the aware businessperson.

The selection of the product or service to offer must reflect your technical knowledge and personal experience. And it had better be a business for which a need exists and from the use of that product or service a benefit can be derived.

For example: Consider the energy crunch. Think of the boom in insulation sales, the expanded (and expanding) opportunities in solar energy. How about pollution control (for autos, smokestacks, whole communities, or whatever)?

There aren't many calls these days for quarterstaves and armor, but there is a constant demand for new goods and services. What you need is the wit to discover the opportunity and the courage to seize the moment.

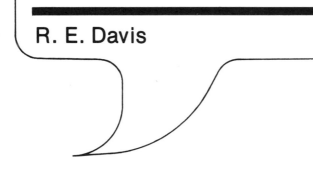

Small companies must be lean and spartan to survive . . . and innovative to prosper.

R. E. Davis

Marketing New Product Ideas

Seeing a new idea slide down the ways—and then float like a cork—is an exciting prospect. First make sure your design is a good one, though; you'd hate to see it sink just when your hopes are highest.

Answer these questions with logic, honesty, thoroughness and emotional detachment:

1. Will the new product benefit the consumer or fill a need?
2. Is this the right time to introduce your widget to a waiting world?
3. Can it be made and sold at a price people will pay—and that will give you a reasonable profit?
4. Should you patent your product? (I'll answer for you. Probably not; it's an expensive process which takes time and alerts anyone else doing work in the same area.)
5. What competition will it have in the marketplace?

6. Who will buy it? Where are they? How can they be reached?

If you can answer these questions and are still not out of hope, money and patience, here's the next sequence:

1. Have samples and prototypes produced.
2. Ditto for brochures and any other descriptive materials. (Do a *good* job here; you want something more sophisticated than a snapshot taken in front of the garage door.)
3. Now the big decision: Will you manufacture your product yourself? Large corporations have established procedures for following up new product ideas, and most of them are good at this phase of endeavor. Do not make the common mistake of going it alone if you can possibly get help at this level.
4. Try to work out a lump sum payment or royalty agreement and let your source take it from there.
5. Don't waste time being paranoid over the possibility that someone will steal your ideas.
6. We warned you, don't fritter away your time and money in patent search and obtaining patents. There's a good reason: In 90 percent of the cases, people who copy patented devices (violators) are not in any way hampered by the patent. Enforcing the laws is difficult and expensive to boot. When you file your patent, you really alert the potential copycats to how you do it. Why lay out

time and money on such foolishness?
Forget it!

If you can't (or decide not to) make a hitch
with a manufacturer, launching a new
product means launching a new business
—going it completely on your own.

You can swim without water
wings—that's what this book is all
about—but the biggest single problem is
usually adequate market representation.
Look in the Yellow Pages for "Rep Finders".
You won't be able to afford your own sales
force to start, so get the best counsel you
can find in your industry. Success or failure
rides on marketing choices, so make the
best decisions you can.

Shyness

A question most frequently asked at my seminars is, "How much should I pay my lawyer (accountant, consultant, etc.)?"

You ask!

And you ask up front.

A reputable professional will not charge for the initial consultation until fee structure is arranged and understood.

No one should be charged for calling on a professional to find out charges and areas of competence and interest. And you can tell them I said so.

So cast aside your coyness and ask, "how much?"

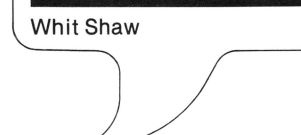

Write your own job description before attempting to write those of your employees . . .

Whit Shaw

How Hard Should You Work?

Or perhaps, "How hard do you have to work?" Or even better, "How hard do you want to work?"

The buck will stop (and start) with you. Certainly there will be long hours. Will they be fun? Would you rather be doing that than the stuff they talk about in *Sports Illustrated?*

It boils down to some pretty fundamental philosophical views of how you want to live. How big a family (or mortgage or ego) do you have to support? What are you proving to yourself, your family and associates?

It's your little red wagon—how heavy do you want to load it?

Just be sure you make your choice when you *have* a choice. When you get your master's license as a tug captain, it's a hell of a time to realize you don't like water.

And the lion shall lie down with the lamb . . . but the lamb won't get much sleep . . .

Anon.

You Deserve a Break Today

A franchise is the granted right to engage in business using another's marketing system and (usually) goods. Of course there is more to it than that; franchising is big business and probably no two franchising systems are exactly the same.

If you say "franchise", someone else immediately says "McDonald's" or "Burger King." Certainly the Big M—and its competitors for the fast-food buck—are the best known in what is a relatively new field.

But there are some 200,000 service stations in the United States, and about three-fourths of them are franchised. And there are more than 30,000 franchised car and truck dealerships. Those two sections of the auto industry together make up about two-thirds of the business (retail dollars) done by U. S. franchisees.

Franchising extends to distributorships, retail stores, service businesses, manufacturing and beyond.

Is franchising for you? Not if you want to be a general, for you'll have to take orders. A few franchisees make it big, but a greater number fail. And maybe you can't meet the beginning requirements—some franchises cost hundreds of thousands of dollars. The only way to learn is to check it out, starting with the franchise agreement:

1. *Initial costs.* Some franchises, such as service stations, have no initial costs; service businesses may charge for their name and / or operating methods. With motels and restaurants, the sky's the limit. Who owns the land, the building, the equipment? Other initial costs might include a site evaluation fee, building construction costs, equipment or furnishing costs. And don't forget your needs for working capital (to run the business with until you start making a profit).
2. *Royalties.* Typically the franchisee will pay a service charge or royalty ranging from 2 to 14 percent of gross sales. He may also be committed to additional monies for advertising.
3. *Territory.* The franchisor will probably have done a feasibility study on the area, and you should too (particularly if he knows less about the location than you). He or you may own the real estate (or he may lease it and sub-lease to you).
4. *Training.* Usually the agreement (especially with the better franchisors) will stipulate training, and may include

periodic on-the-job assistance and advice.

5. *Operation.* The franchisor will retain control to a high degree over your daily operation. He will set rules by which you run the business. (This is a common area of dissatisfaction to franchisees; they often cite inefficient procedures or apathetic support.) Check this out carefully—with other franchisees if you possibly can.

6. *Duration and termination.* A few franchises are for perpetuity, others are for a year only. Just be sure that any side clauses you sign (say, to lease building and equipment) are for the same timespan as the main agreement.
Look carefully at the termination clause. Franchisors insist on their right to cancel in order to maintain their company image, and of course this clause has been abused. Since the termination clause deals with how, when or why you might have to give up your business (and with what you might have left in your pockets), you are well advised to study it and get the best legal advice you can. The termination clause also will spell out any transfer or buy-back provisions.

Use reasonable caution in dealing with the franchisor. There are good ones and there are some whose practices are questionable. But most of them come to the table with a higher level of business sophistication than you do, so just watch it.

"Advertise! Advertise! That's always been your answer to everything."

Advertising, for the Folks Who Can't Brush after Every Meal

You advertise only to:

1. Promote customer awareness of your business, goods or services.
2. Stimulate sales directly, or
3. Establish or change (improve) your image in the public eye.

Decide on your specific goals and what you can spend to pursue a consistent ad program—and the word *consistent* is the key. You will soon discover that it's easy to nickel-and-dime yourself to death with a few little ads here and a few more there. You'll also learn that the big kids on the block don't just charge nickels and dimes, either. So you must have a plan.

Repeat your ads. I say *repeat your ads.* Long after you tire of the message it's just beginning to dawn on customers. There are only two ways to boost your share of what's out there: take business away from the competition, or expand the market. (You could also just boost your prices, but let's stick to advertising for now.)

FACT ONE: You probably don't need an advertising agency.

FACT TWO: You probably should visit several and pick their brains.

FACT THREE: You probably can't afford an agency anyway.

Agency people love the challenge of setting out the right course for an advertiser, but unless you can/will commit to spending at least fifty grand a year, even the little agencies will shrug you off. Since an agency lives on 15 percent of its customers' billings it will naturally head for the big accounts.

Herewith a baker's dozen of tips for the do-it-yourselfer:

1. Avoid cutesie logos made from your and/or your spouse's initials. Save the wit for your license plates.
2. Always print black on white (by far the most frequently used composition in the world).
3. Strive for continuity of message, and know who you're trying to reach.
4. Newspapers are the favorite (most used) medium, have fine graphic potential and "clip out" capability. They might also be the least expensive in your case.
5. Newspapers also have editorial and PR potential. (See PR section)
6. Shopping guides are coming on strong in some markets.

7. In buying radio time consider (a) station format and (b) frequency necessary for sufficient exposure. You pick the air times, rather than take the run-of-the-mill station spots. Forget promotional packages grouped with others; trust your own ads and instincts.

8. Television is expensive. Here you can consider tying in with a supplier or regional distributor. Often late night time periods are cheap, but don't even think about it if your message won't reach the right buyers then.

9. Trade and national magazines now have regional and state editions with a consequent reduction in ad rates. Classified ads may be a lot cheaper too. But remember: They're not a bargain unless your message reaches the right people. That's the name of the game and that's why the Montana Turkey Breeders' Gazette carries very few ads for tuxedo rental services.

10. Look for your own unique selling proposition. Why are you (or your product) different? When you spot your extra something, stress it!

11. If you advertise in different media, use similar campaigns and reap synergistic effects $(1 + 1 = 3)$.

12. The cheapest advertising you can do (effective too) is right on your own property. Use a little flair in your signs and keep your business property neat and spruce.

13. *The very finest advertising is word of mouth,* and it goes without price. You cannot buy it. You must earn it, but once you do—and continue to—it's free.

*The less complex a business is,
the fewer things can go wrong.
The more complex a business is,
the more difficult it is to figure
out what went wrong.*

Peter F. Drucker

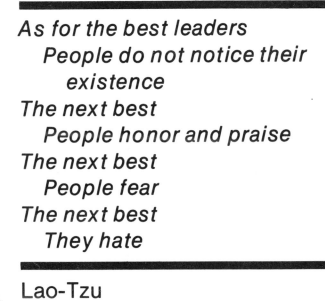

As for the best leaders
   People do not notice their
      existence
The next best
   People honor and praise
The next best
   People fear
The next best
   They hate

Lao-Tzu

"Small Is Beautiful"

In his well-thought-out and well-received book, *Small is Beautiful,* E. F. Schumacher sums up:

"In small-scale enterprise, private ownership is natural, fruitful and just . . . In large-scale enterprise, private ownership is a fiction for the purpose of enabling functionless owners to live parasitically on the labor of others."

So we small businessmen are the beautiful ones, engaged in the pure exercise of capitalism, practicing "economics as if people mattered." There is little that is objectionable or socially disruptive in our small-scale activity.

(An interesting sidelight is that as a group, small businessmen do as well or better for themselves materially and in life styles as their tycoon counterparts who are pummeled from all quarters by a vengeful society bent on nationalizing, collectivizing, limiting and controlling their activities.)

Mother Loves You

Our own Ma Bell is the best gal on the street. Just try to do business telephoning on any scale in Western Europe and you'll quickly see what I mean. Anywhere else, forget it.

Four lessons that seem difficult for the small businessperson to learn:

1. Answer your own phone directly whenever possible, thus avoiding a secretary who protects you from the public and doesn't care what she sounds like doing it. Place your own calls too.
2. Don't waste time on this little game: "I called him first and left a message, so I have to wait for his call." How silly! Call again, repeatedly if you have to, to reach your client.
3. Call anyone, any place, any time. If you have a simple, direct proposition to discuss with the president of a huge company, or the prime minister of an emerging nation, or a potential customer

you've never been able to land, call 'em up! They'll talk with you. Never have others call on your behalf. Don't call an underling. Don't have your secretary call. Simply do it yourself; it works.

4. Constantly update your personal and business phone system. Technology is moving with the speed of light in this area, so check up on the latest gadgetry . . . frequently.

Trust Me Till Friday

Don't carry accounts receivable unless you have to. Many don't have to (Ye Olde Antique Shoppe, Joe's Eats). Thousands of others have eliminated their receivables and use major credit cards.

If you *must* extend credit, some points:

1. Have the person who extends credit for you be responsible for its collection. That is a neat combination of responsibility and authority, and it really works.
2. Keep an eye on losses from bad debts. If they're large, the answer is obviously to tighten up. But if they're non-existent, perhaps you're missing a chance to make a buck. It's possible you should reach out more.
3. When it comes to billing, the early bird gets the worm. If your competitors send out their bills on the 1st of the month (as most do) send yours out on the 25th.
4. Be liberal—even unique—in your terms and discounts. A better deal to en-

courage early payment (if it's good enough to work) really amounts to an economy for you. Your money can't help you while it's in a customer's pocket.

5. Write your credit policy down and make sure that the people administering it understand it with crystal clarity. Allow no exceptions.

If you do deal with the purveyors of plastic money, apply pressure now and then to get a decrease in your discount rate. Regardless of what they say, there is *not* a single rate for all. The volume of business is an important factor to be sure, but so is the average size of each charge.

A discussion of rates may save you one to one and a half percent of your charge sales, and what's wrong with that? Dun & Bradstreet, the largest of the organizations in the credit business (have you ever been dunned for money?) will call on you sooner or later. D & B offers many services which you may or may not need; and of course it isn't in business for its health any more than you are. There is a free package of introductory services.

Dun & Bradstreet will rate you (as a credit risk) whether you subscribe to its services or not. Yes, Virginia, a high D & B rating is a Good Thing.

Help! Help!

The smaller the business the more important each person is. Good employees probably are your greatest asset; finding, training and keeping them may well be your greatest source of headaches.

First, consider not hiring at all.

Can you do it yourself, at least for a while? Think about giving up that month of Sundays. Surely you're more efficient at the task you need help with than any new employee would be, and you're already on hand and trained. And better motivated. And cheaper.

If that doesn't work and you *do* need help, think about temporaries from an agency. Unless you are really located off in Paul Bunyan country, you can get office help at least. It ain't cheap but you don't have employer-type headaches. If you need help with low-skill grunt work, try the local high school. Or pool hall.

Is the workload in your firm distributed equitably? Perhaps you could delegate extra

Hire from outside

"*I've heard that outside of working hours he's really a rather decent sort.*"

tasks to a non-productive employee. (You say you don't have one? May I come shake your hand?) Are you sure you need to get the new task done at all? Maybe you could just eliminate it. Figure another way of accomplishing the same end by using different means.

Hire an outside contractor. You won't save money by bringing all your technicians in on a Saturday morning to help you landscape your new office.

If the decision is to hire:

First, write a job description, including duties, needed background and the employee's place in the company hierarchy. Describe fringe benefits, salary range and outlook for advancement. Don't be flowery; you aren't writing it for any reason except to be understood.

Promote from inside

Lastly, promote from within if it is humanly possible—and it usually is. Such a policy is the best way of letting other employees know that you appreciate good efforts on your behalf.

One last thought on employment and small business: *You can't compete with the Fortune 500 firms when it comes to fringe benefits.* You will have to pay higher salaries or accept inferior help. The former is disagreeable but the latter is intolerable, so be prepared to shell out an additional 5 or even 10 percent in salary.

How to Cross the Swamp Without Getting Your Feet Wet

Let's say you have a nice little tile-and-carpet business. Some of your customers do it themselves, but of course most of them can't. You need an installer.

But you can't afford to have carpet installers hanging about on your time when there isn't any carpet to install. What to do?

Draw up an agreement like this:

"It is my understanding that I am to be retained by Reggie's Rugs, Inc., as an independent contractor for the installation of floor covering material and related services. Reggie's Rugs, Inc., will pay me an agreed contract price and I understand that I will be responsible for my own federal and state taxes, social security, insurance, etc.

SEEN AND AGREED

by_____, President
   Reggie's Rugs, Inc."

Simple and foolproof.

119

To be considered as an independent contract employee, an individual must (among other requirements):

1. own his own tools, if any
2. work without direct controlling supervision (minute by minute)
3. somewhat determine his own hours and/or sequence of jobs
4. not be otherwise treated as a salaried employee (i.e., given benefits, etc.)

It is an area of potential savings for an employer under the right circumstances, but *should be approached with caution* and the best advice available.
An excellent report is available from:

U.S. General Accounting Office
Distribution Section, Room 4522
441 G Street N.W.
Washington, D.C. 20548

Report to the Joint Commission on Taxation, Congress of the U.S., by the Comptroller General of the U.S. - Tax treatment of employees and self-employed persons by the I.R.S. Problems and solutions.

A Super Source of Assistance —the Rep

Some of the most interesting guys in business today are the reps, the business representatives.

Essentially, they are salesmen, working for small mid-sized companies which simply cannot afford a network sales office. These nice folks are often in the third or fourth generation of hustling products.

They are honest and hard-working small businessmen themselves, and most of them are extremely fast on their feet. They represent a vast source of knowledge and market information in just about every conceivable product line. They can help you advertise, find prospects, price your product and decide when, where and how to test the market.

And you usually pay the rep only when he sells something for you. Only rarely will a rep warehouse a product for you, though; that's the function of a distributor (or you, if you don't have a distributor).

The rep is constantly looking for people like you, who want help to move a hot new product. A rep, for your particular needs, can be reached directly through a rep finder or recruited by a management consultant.

I find most reps to be extroverted, hard-working, natural partners for the emerging business entrepreneur.

Migod, Is It Noon Already?

As you know, people have energy peaks during the day, and also corresponding valleys. Lyndon Johnson took a nap after lunch every day (presumably sleeping soundly with the knowledge that the country was in good hands).

And what does this mean to you?

Well, if your business is small enough so your habits don't affect other people, and if it's of a type in which customers don't clog up your day, operate it whenever you like. A lobsterman goes to work before dawn but you don't have to. If you're a commercial artist, say, and you feel creative at midnight, go to it.

IT'S NOT CHISELED IN STONE ANYWHERE THAT YOU MUST WORK FROM 9 TO 5 MONDAY TO FRIDAY.

Executive Stress

You're a prime candidate for stress if you:

1. Are always fighting time, scheduling more than you or your aides can handle.
2. Expect your employees to share your goals.
3. Expect more acclaim than you get (from above or below).
4. Feel trapped in your position, either under- or over-prepared.
5. Feel caught outside your behavior limits, doing things you dislike.

You know the signs of stress: aggressive behavior and reaction, impatience, annoyance, loud tone of voice. Normal amounts of tension are constructive, but stress is not, and it destroys relationships and attitudes and demoralizes your work force.

It's not good for your blood pressure, either. Sit back and rethink things every now and then, particularly if you start to notice danger signs in yourself.

A Person of High Degree

39

If you hold a MBA (or even worse, a business/economics doctorate) from a prestigious Eastern school, congratulations! I'm sure Mom and Dad are proud.

This kind of accomplishment, however, is no help for you in 90 percent of small business. What is usually lacking in an MBA is humility, understanding of entrepreneurial functions, guts, and willingness to work long hours for a long time in order to succeed.

The best graduate schools carefully train their progeny to step gracefully into a role as a captain of industry. These fledglings will tolerate only the briefest of sojourns at dignified and sweatless labor in the vineyard before elegantly donning the mantle of chief executive officer.

If you are an MBA, there's not much this author can do . . .

But for lord's sake, don't hire one!

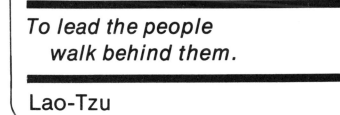

To lead the people
  walk behind them.

Lao-Tzu

If a Chameleon Can Do It, Why Can't You?

Ralph Waldo Emerson said that "Adaptability is the hallmark of a mature personality."

To have staying power in entrepreneurial activities, you must be able to adapt successfully to the needs of clients, customers, associates, employees, suppliers—everyone you deal with, in other words.

YOU MUST LEARN TO BE ALL THINGS TO ALL MEN.

Different people must be handled differently, and people-handling is a strategic (and challenging and fun) part of your game plan for profit.

As you enter business, remember the bad practices you complained about as a customer . . . and don't repeat them!

Whit Shaw

Truth in Business (And Other Unnatural Practices)

 Complete truthfulness is a wonderful sales technique.

It may not amaze you, but it certainly would surprise many businessmen to learn that full and open disclosure and discussion of unfavorable aspects of a sale is an effective marketing tool.

If you ignore or gloss over your widget's bad points, your avoidance is doubtless obvious to the prospect. Truthfully pointing out alternate courses of action (other than those which would benefit you) is so refreshing that it will help you close the sale on the spot.

Example: The most successful automobile dealer I ever knew trained his used car salespeople to point out at least one defect, *before* the customer saw it, in every demonstration of an otherwise spotless "creampuff." It worked for him; it will work for you.

Doing business during the current high tide of consumerism is really not very difficult. The only real hazard is the bureaucrat; so follow carefully the prescribed regulations, particularly if you grant credit or sell on conditional terms.

The recent flood of regulations has done little or nothing to "protect" the consumer or to alter buying habits.

Plenty of people will buy all the goods and services you can possibly sell, if you *give them service and tell it like it is!*

What to Do Till the Union Comes

Most small businessmen look forward to the coming of a labor union the way Marie Antoinette looked forward to her first ride in a tumbrel.

There are several excellent books on the subject that will forestall cold sweats and abject panic. For the present you should review how the troops are being treated. You should:

1. Pay five percent above the going wage in the area for the job.
2. Provide some sort of incentive for performance at every level.
3. Promote from within wherever possible.
4. Weed the ranks frequently for trouble-makers and freeloaders.

This should give you the top folks and enable you to keep them. Care and attention to this can postpone your next NLRB hearing . . . perhaps forever.

Retreads

Old retired big-company tycoons are of little help to you. It's fine to listen to their advice, but *don't hire them.* You can't afford the fat cat with his impressive resume.

Also stay away from retired armed services types—don't even listen to their advice. They're light years away from you in basic goals. To be successful in the armed services, it is necessary that one develop a multitude of bad habits, any one of which would scuttle your business. (Besides, that nice fat pension they're getting—and you're paying for—has a tendency to, uh, emasculate their ambitions.)

Then, of course, there's SCORE, the Service Corps of Retired Executives. They work mostly from referrals by the SBA. Many of these fine old gentlemen were in small businesses like yours. Their services are free, very often can be helpful, and you must agree the price is right.

Another bright note; professional management consulting groups of retirees with

specific small business backgrounds are
now operating in many areas. Check around.

Intrigue on the Orient Express

I personally love the challenge of offshore business, and have dabbled in small diverse ventures which permit me a couple of weeks' skiing (and *gemütlichkeit*) in the Austrian Tyrol each March; "necessary" visitations to the azure Antilles (with tennis gear packed) and regular tender-loving-care to little efforts in other far-flung watering holes.

The day has long passed when any American business person should feel ill at ease pursuing an enterprise anywhere in the world. "American" is the *lingua franca* of business, export, import. Sell your goods or services, and be at ease; the entire world is your marketplace.

Hints:

1. Take much time to seek expert and reputable assistance in your projects. You must be endlessly circumspect, for each area of the world has its own perils.
2. Always limit your exposure, reduce your up front commitments, negotiate for advance payments, minimize risks.

3. Before thinking of business, learn about the customs, practices and the people with whom you will deal.
4. Always start *very small and very slowly.* There are many eloquent talkers—and accents—in international trade; you're just a country boy, remember.
   (I wish I had the time in this thin volume for a few tales of international intrigue . . . perhaps in the next.)
5. Take lots of time and get much exposure and many second opinions before choosing the final outlet for your genius. If things don't suit you *exacty,* look elsewhere!
6. Work at learning at least a smattering of the native tongue in your area of choice.

Until the magic moment, then, *bonne chance! und glückliche reise!*

Wheeler-Dealers

As a small businessman you will spend a lot of time, effort and money on company cars and trucks, so you might as well do it right. The savings are immense.

Herewith Shaw's Laws:

1. Never, but never, trade cars/trucks with your friendly dealer.
2. Consider leasing.
3. Match the vehicle to the job.

Let me expand on these points, in order:

Never trade cars or trucks. When you are finished with your rusty chariot, sell it yourself in the retail market. (Your local dealer, Ralph the Ripoff Artist, will pay you only a wholesale price for your trade-in, despite what he says).

Sell it yourself

Selling it yourself is easy, really. Look up the vehicle's top retail value as found in any of several regional guides published monthly (NADA, Blue Book, Red Book, etc.—your banker has one), add 100 dollars, then round upward to the nearest "ninety-five" dollar mark. If you haven't hung on to your little jewel *too* long, you won't have to adjust for excessive mileage or obvious cosmetic or mechanical deficiencies. Clean and wax your old steed, even if you didn't when you were using it; the time and money will be well repaid.

Advertise in your local newspaper, nowhere else. Keep your ad short, simple, informative. *Always* include the price, and the words "low mileage" and "exceptionally clean." Don't be coy with box numbers; include your name, address and an all-hours telephone number. (In other words, make it easy for the buyer to buy.) The response should be a pleasant surprise, and closing the sale is easy. The customer knows the price and has come to you, so obviously he wants to buy. The ritual is the same whether you're selling ten-wheelers or economy sedans. Let them (1) look it over, (2) try it out (with you in the other seat of course) and (3) close the sale.

If you happen to have several units—or one expensive one—ask your banker beforehand if he'll lend a hand with the financing.

And buy for cash

Now you're ready to buy your new units for cash. Make your choice of manufacturer, model and specifications and stick with it. See at least three different dealers. The average markup is roughly 25 percent on full size cars and trucks, 20 percent on inter-mediate and economy models and as low as 15 percent on some small domestic and foreign subcompacts.

All dealers pay about the same for their cars. The largest dealer gets no price break. "Vehicle buying services" are *no help.* Forget them.

But note: the dealer gets an additional five percent back from the manufacturer for "holdovers" (cars on his lot when the new models come out) and another two percent "holdback" or "incentive."

Some more hints:

1. Don't keep company cars more than two years or 40,000 miles.
2. Allow the dealer a profit of eight to ten percent and you can do business.
3. Talk with the dealer himself; don't just wander onto the lot and find the nearest salesman.
4. Buy a popular color (red is great) to enhance resale.
5. Take full advantage of the manufacturer's warranty.
6. Review service and maintenance costs often and carefully.

Maybe leasing is the answer for you. It has these advantages:

1. Your cash stays in the bank.
2. Your "rolling stock" budget can be determined.
3. Your tax accountability is simpler.
4. You don't pay vehicle overhead (sometimes the lease arrangement can cover repairs, maintenance, service and insurance).

5. You get more insurance for less, usually through the leasing company's grouping and volume.

There are disadvantages to leasing, and they all boil down to this: in the long run *leasing costs more*. (Because you pay the profit for the leasing company. And the longer the term of the lease, the more profit.)

The big boys say, "Buy what appreciates and lease what depreciates." Vehicles do indeed depreciate. There are a few cases in which that isn't true, but then you aren't going to deliver your bologna in a Bugatti, are you?

Matching the vehicle to your job requirements requires only a modicum of common sense and can be done in a few minutes a day, right in the privacy of your home. No dunce would deliver an armful of yellow freesias in a dump truck, but why invest in a panel truck if all you have to deliver is dental plates or pizzas?

Just remember that if you make the wrong choice you'll be reminded of it every day for a couple of years.

S-x at the Water Cooler

46

Don't.

If you feel you *must* demonstrate your, uh, magnetism, the office or plant is the worst possible place to do it.

In the first place, everyone will know. And talk. You may think your little affair is fine and good and true, but to everyone else it (and you) are just silly. Their esteem for you will certainly fall.

Besides, what will you do when the Grand Passion has withered? Fire your ex-bedmate?

Better by far to follow that fine old advice from someone or other in the Broadway hit, *How to Succeed in Business Without Really Trying,* "a secretary is not an erector set."

Being Caught in the Act of Doing Something Good

Your public relations image in the business community usually takes care of itself (you get what you deserve). To receive favorable public notice you must:

1. Be newsworthy, or
2. Structure so as to appear to be newsworthy.

In any case, never make the common error of using leverage to ask a customer for paid advertising to buy your way into news or editorial columns. Even if it works (it usually doesn't) it will fool no one, and you'll make all the local influential news molders think of you as a dink.

Instead, an excellent ploy is to let the news people (of whichever medium) "discover" you. You will be amazed at the attention you will get. Carefully selected good works of a visible sort are helpful to the cause, particularly in the smaller communities.

Good works work

It will cost you a hell of a lot less to give the Girl Scouts three trees to plant on Arbor Day than it will to take an ad telling the town that you're a great guy. It will do you a hell of a lot more good, too.

Besides, even if no one were to hear about it, it would still be a Good Thing.

Physical Fitness

Heaven knows, you've got to be tough to make it these days. You know the killers as well as I do:

1. Overeat.
2. Smoke constantly.
3. Lotsa booze.
4. No exercise (except on weekends, and then lots to catch up).

A sense of well-being radiates from the person in fine physical condition. Get yourself into the proper mental attitude to build your stamina now. Tennis, swimming, handball, gymnastics, jogging, are great, and so are dozens of others.

Commit yourself to a certain schedule; it's the only way you'll do it regularly. You have nothing to lose but your pot.

Stop Thief!

American small businesses lost an estimated 20 billion dollars to criminals last year. And those are just "reported" thefts, the tip of the iceberg.

If you're being burgled (or don't want to be) try one or more of these fixes:

1. Secure locks on all doors and windows.
2. Strict key control system.
3. Tempered glass, iron screens, grilles, etc.
4. Bright lights.
5. Co-op patrols and/or watch dogs.
6. Frequent bank deposits.
7. Insurance update.
8. A good alarm system.

There are many new and good alarm systems:

1. Silent alarm (rings at the police station).
2. Perimeter protection (on doors and windows).
3. Ultrasonic.

4. Microwave.
5. Photoelectric.
6. Sound-sensitive.
7. Pressure-sensitive.
8. Shock-sensitive.
9. Capacitance alarm.

If the wide range of types and costs bewilders you (and it's understandable), local law enforcement agencies will be glad to steer you to the reputable companies nearby.

Shop several; it's a specialized field. Ask where their systems are installed in your neighborhood and check each out with the owner first-hand.

Or sell something heavy

It's easy to eliminate shoplifting; just sell something that's too heavy to carry. If this is impractical, try the usual deterrents: mirrors, locked cases, one-way viewers, attentive salespeople, tamper-proof tags, alert cashiers. They all help.

The best solution is an enthusiastic and visible apprehension and prosecution, with full publicity. A little of this, and shoplifters will take their custom to other stores— exclusively.

Know your laws, and follow up on their full enforcement. No room for goody-two-shoes here.

Hallelujah! Born Again!

Investigate seminars, symposiums, clinics, conferences, and workshops tailored to your particular needs (and if you have any, to your weaknesses).

Many are sponsored by the U. S. Department of Commerce, the SBA, the American Management Association and varied colleges and universities; and, boy, are they dull.

The really zingy ones are led by "gypsies," generally from the business or financial community. These presentations can be pragmatic as hell, fundamentalist in delivery, and entertaining to boot. If the subject matter hits you where you live, you'll go home with half a dozen ideas to try, and you'll have been provoked to think from a fresh perspective.

Most of these entrepreneurs will go into their act for two or three consecutive nights, often with local sponsorship. Such workshops can be profitably conducted in any community—perhaps yours.

Note: It may not surprise you to learn that this has been Yr. Ftfl. Svnt.'s favorite activity for years; seminars are as much fun to give as to attend!

Salesmanship

The best salesperson I ever met (at an executive meeting in Philadelphia several years ago) was:

1. Black
2. Female
3. Over forty
4. Poorly educated; hadn't finished high school
5. Short and fat
6. Nearly blind
7. Less than articulate

She sold life insurance in a low-income section of South Philadelphia for a top ten company—several million dollars worth that year—and was national sales leader.

She was an impressive person, and her lesson was obvious: Work with what you've got; you're not going to undergo a magic transformation. Don't mope about waiting for the princess to stop and kiss an ugly frog like you. The princess may be slow in coming.

Twenty per cent of any group of salesmen will always produce 80 per cent of the sales.

Peter Townsend

Selling Your Product

The esteemed dean of business writers, Peter Drucker, tells us, "We are now entering into an era of emphasis on the entrepreneur." Profitable sales are indeed the lifeblood of any business—large or small—and the people and companies good at selling are the most successful in the business community. It's as simple as that.

Is there a flawless sales system? Well, yes and no. *No* system can be flawless, however, *yes* has to be the answer for those who can relate to the following hints and techniques.

Involve yourself with functions of time. Within these time frames be productive (not just busy), taking a moment to consider good basic selling habits and how best to form them into *your own flawless system.* That's the key, and your first step to selling success. Here's how to go about it: *All selling success is comprised of three basics; work, personality and technical knowledge.* (Sure, that is simplistic, but bear with me). Let's start with the first and—since these areas blend with one another—plow on to the end.

Expose
yourself

You must reach out for more exposure. Obviously if you make more calls and your percentage of closing remains the same, your total sales will go up. Make the law of averages work for you. To make those extra calls, you must organize your efforts. Remember that the more independent from supervision you are, the more self-disciplined you must be.

Set up a three-by-five file card system with tabs from front to back labeled today, tomorrow, one through 31, and A to Z. On the front of each customer card record the name of the company, its purchasing agent or contact, addresses, phone numbers and product category.

On the back, list current and potential volume, personalities you deal with at the firm, history, call frequency, problems, objectives, competitors, strategies, and anything else that seems germane.

Constantly rotate the file by bringing your monthly workload from the A to Z section into the day of the month section and rotate this to give weekly or daily objectives.

This is your Automatic Memory System. Simple as it may seem, the AMS works and you must use it. Don't trust your headbone.

If you have a geographical territory, manage it rather than let it manage you. Pre-qualify prospects when you have the experience to do so; it's a great time-saver.

Sales prospecting can be defined as the best way to zero in on clients/opportunities with maximum efficiency. You will thus shorten your work time-frames and be more productive. You must remember: *ALWAYS SELL THE BENEFITS.*

Sell the benefits

You sell usually to either of two groups (sometimes both): to the consumer (who uses your product or service), or to trade (which resells your product or service for profit). So when you stress the benefits, remember that the buyer sees them differently. To the consumer, the benefit is a better product or service; to the trade, the benefit is greater profit.

There will of course be dead time, and the more there is, the less productive you can be. *Constantly strive to reduce dead time.* A few tips:

1. The 5-10-5 system (five letters, ten phone calls, five live calls every day).
2. Automatic Memory System. Keep it updated.
3. Observe your client's surroundings.
4. "The daily ten," in order of importance. (A pocket list.)
5. Do expense accounts.
6. Prepare mentally for the next call.
7. Resolve to listen more carefully.
8. Change—or at least think about—your sales presentation.
9. Get promotional tools in order.
10. Phone, don't write.
11. A letter should contain one idea and a request for action.

157

12. Learn to read faster.
13. Bank by mail.
14. Use car cassettes or a recorder.
15. Set fewer meetings—and those for good cause only.

Let's move to the second side of the work-personality-knowledge triangle. What you get out of any job depends not only on the quantity of effort you put into it (work) but also the quality, and that's a reflection of your personality.

Selling may be compared to playing tennis: if you hit a lot of balls into the court you will eventually win points, games, and matches. If you hit more you will win more, so persistence is obviously important. Listen to what Abe Lincoln had to say about persistence (and the law of averages):

"I will do the very best I know how—the very best I can; and I mean to keep doing so until the end. If the end brings me out all right, what is said against me won't amount to anything. If the end brings me out wrong, ten angels swearing I was right would make no difference."

Plod on

It is smart to be industrious. Sometimes we allow a man to be ridiculed by calling him a plodder, the implication being that he is a little stupid. In fact, every great man is a plodder in the sense that he works patiently and enthusiastically day after day, confident that in the end he will succeed. Talent alone is not enough; nothing is more common than an unsuccessful man with talent, the classic "underachiever."

158

Only three years before he won the United States Open Tennis championship, Stan Smith was considered too awkward to be used as a ball boy! And Beethoven, even though he was deaf late in his life, was still writing great music.

J. C. Penney said, "Success in life does not depend on genius. Any young man of ordinary intelligence who is not afraid of work should succeed in spite of obstacles and handicaps if he plays the game fairly and squarely and keeps at it."

Now do you believe me?

Some suggestions on developing persistence:

1. Make a game of completing small tasks.
2. Accept the fact that some duties are necessary.
3. Consult the top salesman.
4. Do the ornery job first.
5. Note that in many sales areas the sale is not consummated until the fourth or fifth call.

Another personality trait that is indispensable is personal excitement or enthusiasm about the product. Hell, if *you* don't think it's the best there is, what are you doing making and selling it?

Fire up!

Enthusiasm in selling is contagious. Keep the buyer talking, bridge his obligations, let your enthusiasm inflame him. The secret ingredient is you; when you learn that, sales miracles will happen!

To complete the foundation that will give you optimum confidence in your sales ability, let's touch on technical knowledge.

To begin with, of course, you have to *know your product*—its capabilities, uses, benefits, weaknesses, its dimensions, color options, parts availability, and anything and everything else that pertains to it.

One would have thought from ads that FoMoCo was selling the tailgates on its station wagons a few years ago (and so it was). The airlines don't stress that their fares are exactly the same as everyone else's; Pan Am talks exclusively about its experience; SAS plugs its on-board food (!) and others talk of the quality of their inflight movies. Do you know more about marketing than they do?

Tie in closely with other established items, perhaps even a competitor's. Removing the unknown element might well be the key to sales.

Demonstrate if possible.

Does your new item *do it better/do it easier/cost less?* Stress the benefits!

Don't knock the competition, don't argue, don't criticize. Above all don't ridicule.

Don't discount the customer's desire to be the *first* in his group/club/business/area to own your product. Snob appeal still works—just ask the guys who sell for Coors Beer.

Plug your warranty.

Forget the past, live in the present. As in tennis (can you tell I love the game?), the only shot that counts is the next one. Certainly you should profit from past experience, but look ahead. There are some warning signs that tell us that the unconscious need to fail may be acting up. For instance:

1. We forget appointments.
2. We knock off early.
3. We tackle only the easiest customers.
4. We are contemptuous of our superiors.
5. We reject offers of help.
6. We collect grievances (he loused me up and I'm not going to forget it).
7. We have a reason for everything that goes wrong (and that reason exonerates us).
8. We resent the successful (but never try to take a leaf from their book).

Anyone can have a slump. The most gifted and successful people in selling can and do have them. How can you get out of it?

1. Make things more pleasant for yourself. Buy something new. Get your briefcase in order, get your car cleaned up. Buy a new suit.
2. Ask yourself a few tough questions: Am I calling on really qualified prospects? Do I plan each call as well as I can? Am I ducking the toughies? Why did I lose that sale last week? How can I correct that situation?
3. Set yourself attainable goals. When you accomplish your objectives, raise them!
4. Review your performance every day, perhaps while on the way home or when relaxing before dinner. Ask yourself: How

did I do today? Did I do what I set out to do? Was I productive or just busy? In what ways did I grow? Am I getting closer to my goals in life? What can I plan tomorrow that will make it even better?

This leads us to what I call the tremendous trifles, the little things that make or break your sales career. They are so personal and trite that I shouldn't have to mention them to an adult, but they are so important that I will anyway:

1. Don't use sloppy or provocative dress.
2. Some people have hair hangups—wear yours conservatively.
3. Fix your teeth—you're not a hockey player.
4. People don't appreciate bad breath.
5. Bathe daily, and make sure your clothes are clean.
6. Mind your eating habits.
7. No one likes a sour expression or a cynical attitude.
8. Use caution if you're a smoker.
9. Keep your fingernails clean.
10. Be realistic.
11. Be modest. No one likes a braggart.
12. Discard mannerisms that annoy, such as yawning or belching.
13. Don't look at your watch.
14. Speak proper English, well modulated and softly.
15. Listen (you have two ears and only one mouth).
16. Be generous in praise.
17. Be courteous.

18. Be friendly and affable, not self-important.
19. Above all, be natural and unaffected.
20. Smile, smile, smile.

These are the tremendous trifles of personal life. There are also tremendous trifles in closing sales:

1. Be punctual.
2. Be brief. (Ask them to buy!)
3. Allow tryouts (that's how they sell puppy dogs and cars).
4. Remember, your customer's time is valuable.
5. Repeat the benefits of your product/service.
6. Stress the guarantee or warranty.
7. How about time sales or credit terms?
8. Offer a color/model choice.
9. Answer any objections point by point.
10. Sign, sign, for God's sake *sign!* (Not autograph or approve.)

Let me end this harangue with a personal anecdote. One of the most successful businessmen I know plays tennis with me, and when I beat him, I always accuse him of being a poor loser. He isn't really. He is a very gracious man who has achieved fantastic results by applying the principles embodied in this chapter.

His response is always the same:

"Whit, I just can't be a good loser, because a good loser is, really, simply a loser, and I haven't had very much practice at being a loser."

Avoid the Pitfalls

 In small business, success or failure often is an extension of the goal-striving ability of the principal (i.e., you).

Winners tend to become bigger winners, and losers seem to show us the same symptoms of trouble time and again. The thirteen follies listed below appear singly or in combination in virtually every small business demise (and some of the big ones):

1. The management belief that extra cash will solve every problem. The most frequently heard excuse is "we failed because of insufficient capital" (but good management is the solution).
2. The pie-in-the-sky or my-ship-will-come-in-any-day-now syndrome. (Sure it will, sonny; and in the meantime who helps cross the street?)
3. A smug management attitude, which downgrades the need for experience and/or expertise in every key job (particularly the one at the top).

165

4. No lines of authority or responsibility. If there isn't an obvious second in command, the ship goes down with the captain.
5. Management reluctance to seek out (and follow) the best business counselors available when problems are evident.
6. Sloppy record-keeping. The businessperson can't be informed if the records are in disarray.
7. Slow-moving, outdated or excessive inventory. Poor buying habits. Not taking advantage of discounts. Difficulty in obtaining credit.
8. Management that fails to plan ahead. Many businesses lose 20 percent of their customers annually; this volume must be replaced.
9. Management that grants credit too leniently, provides over-generous terms, or is lax in collections, will soon be in trouble.
10. Owners who can't delegate (and haven't the hours to do it all themselves) are asking for trouble.
11. Management which is interested in most other aspects of the business except sales and marketing should be suspect.
12. Trouble is surely brewing where human factors are ignored in training, guidance, promotion, airing problems, etc. How you treat people will be a large factor in your success.

13. Management which fails to inspire—or at least provide firm leadership and direction.

If any of this foolishness exists in your operation, it merits top priority attention! NOW!

Sex and Profit

Two unrelated periodicals, the *Wall Street Journal* and the AMA's *Journal of Medicine,* published the findings of a doctorate thesis recently, folks, and the news is good.

According to this scientific study, *SUCCESS in small business is good for your sex life!*

The study, completed over an extended range of time with a wide sampling of participants, *concluded that hard work and neglect of family were problems only when the effort brought little evidence of profit.* The study noted that higher success and profitability in business brought greater satisfaction with the businessperson's own sexual adjustment.

Hallelujah! Try that in your next business plan!

Some people
  sell out and retire from
  their business.
Others
  retire with their business.
But sometimes
  the business retires first!

Whit Shaw

Selling Out

In the first place, I think it is a damn good idea to sell your business occasionally. I don't recommend being a gadfly, but no business should be sacred to you.

First, of course, make sure that you really *do* want to sell. Any good business broker will tell you that about half the time a seller would like to continue in business if the right solutions could be found to his problems—and very often they can.

But you have decided to sell, and you want to do it now. The first question is, is this the right time? Don't wait for a downturn in profits, death, divorce, creditors storming the gates, or the sheriff and the wolf fighting over who gets through the door first. You won't get the kind of lookers you're after.

The time to sell is at "the turn of the curve," just after an upswing (and just before the indicators point to a leveling off).

First, think about selling to someone in the same line, perhaps a relative. Make a low-key approach. If that turns blank, the remaining choices are these:

1. Embark on a campaign yourself to do the job. Sure this means work for you, but you keep the commission money.
2. Hire a commercial realtor. This course is fine if what you're selling is an apartment house, motel, variety store, restaurant, or whatever.
3. Find yourself a competent business broker to do the job right, meaning more dollars in your fist when the dust settles.

The catch is "competent"

There's usually a catch somewhere, and here it is hidden in the word competent.

Start your search by looking in the Yellow Pages, and continue by looking through the financial pages of your newspaper. When you find the announcement of a successful sale, merger or acquisition, pay a visit in person. Check out the references. Ask your banker, ask your lawyer, ask his former clients.

Make sure the firm you choose is thoroughly versed in local problems, and solutions—and *knows your area of business* as well. (If he specializes in selling poultry processing plants, and you make aerospace gizmos, well . . .)

The two of you should draw up an action plan, and this will take more thought than your first glance might show. For instance, your business accounting has been structured to reduce corporate tax liability—and thus would show a dismal record of performance to a prospective buyer. (You say your accounting *hasn't* been so set up? No wonder you want to sell, buddy . . .)

Your broker will help correlate and prepare a realistic business analysis and a projection. Then, the two of you will determine final price considerations and terms and the right (best for you) financial package.

Only then will the broker expose your business to qualified buyers (and/or other brokers) and he will do this on a discreet, confidential and selective basis.

After the buyer is found the broker will lead you through the maze of letters of intent, buy/sell agreements and other closing documents until the sale is final.

Then you can go fishing . . .

One final word: You pick your broker with the same care (and for the same reasons) that you use in picking a banker, lawyer, consultant or accountant. You want his expertise and he has it for sale. *Give him your complete trust and do what he says.*

There are three faithful friends:
an old wife, an old dog, and
ready money.

Ben Franklin
Poor Richard's Almanac

Cases in Point

Many businesses start from common backgrounds. I have had experience leading a few babes out of the woods, and some case histories might be instructive.

The Entrepreneur Who Moved Too Fast: Eddie was a top-notch salesman who suddenly realized (at the age of 40) that OSHA and EPA requirements had killed so many foundries that increased demand for foundry requirements simply was not being met.

So, he started one, used all his savings and brought in equity partners (by dint of his salesmanship). The funds were soon gone and there was still no production. Eddie went to another investor who tied him to a legal agreement which would have cost Eddie the control of his own company.

My solution: Bring in an administrative tiger with a solid business plan and knowledge of financial leverage. Buy out the would-be raider. Implement the business plan. Put Eddie back to what he did best, selling his product.

Now Eddie and his company are prospering nicely, thank you. The moral is obviously to *do what you do best and get help in the other areas.*

The Idea Is Worth More Than the Money: A young horticulturist came to me with a good solid plan for a florist shop and garden center. But he had no money and felt trapped as an employee in a "boob-ordinate" position. I reminded him that debtor's prisons had long since been abolished and had him examine "Who's Who in American Business." (A sturdy percentage of this nation's tycoons have survived brushes with bankruptcy courts on the way to their particular summits.)

We put together a careful package and had it accepted by a government funding program that had never once been used in our state since the program had been established. Not only did my horticulturist get $100,000 to buy his business, he got another $25,000 for operating capital!

His venture has been an outstanding success from the start.

Never be afraid to try.

The Talented Son and the Blind Father: I was called to the office of a mid-sized manufacturing firm with new and modern facilities. The owner, in his early sixties, wanted to unload. His company was well established, profitable and growing.

Our conversation was interrupted by a young man who was introduced as the owner's oldest son, production manager of the firm. When he left, I asked the obvious question. "Would he be interested in the takeover?" The response was that the son, although technically competent, lacked the desire and guts to shoulder the task.

Soon after I placed the business on the market, I was told by the owner's wife that under no circumstances would the business be sold to anyone but her son—and of course it was. All he had needed was the nudge. Did I collect my commission? (Of course, I had earned it. I had provided the nudge.)

Do you remember Poe's *Purloined Letter,* in which a letter was successfully hidden by being put in the most obvious place, a letter rack? Same thing here. If Papa had been a bit more aware, he could have saved effort, money (my commission) and, presumably, a hassle with his wife.

Some situations in business are so ludicrous they scream for help. I recently read of a trio of entrepreneurs who set up a firm to repair camping gear—you rip your tent, they sew it back up. Nice idea, and it should work. But their projected *gross* for a year was $24,000! After you take out three full-time salaries, supplies, rent, utilities and so forth, you could only draw the conclusion they would be better off as galley slaves. They needed help immediately, and obviously they didn't know it.

Moral: *A good idea and blind faith aren't enough.*

Riches appear to me not at all necessary; but competence, I think, is.

Sir Humphrey Davy

I Wax Philosophic

I am occasionally accused of being some-what to the right of Genghis Khan, but I *do* hold these truths self-evident:

1. Most small business types should be allowed to look after themselves, and will do a good job, fairly, if left alone.
2. The same intrigues and satisfactions exist for these people in their business as others find in art, dance, theatre, music, sex, or food.
3. Students, doctors, housewives, laborers, retirees, minorities—all have a chance to put their own resources of mind, time and money into this pursuit, with no guarantees, no promises, no sure thing. It's our "right to fail"—or our license to succeed.

How pleasant it is to have money!

An Entrepreneurial Exam

It is true that we are creatures of conditioned response. How we react to key psychological decisions may give a strong indication of how we will make it on our own in a business situation where the buck stops at our desk.

Here are a few questions based on the thoughts of several business psychologists who have extensively analyzed the essential entrepreneurial characteristics.

These questions will reveal whether or not you have some of those attitudes that are viewed as basic to success in the operation of any small business (or a large one for that matter).

Answer the questions as you really feel. Not every answer will exactly express your feeling—simply pick the one that comes closest. Avoid choosing answers that you feel would be a consensus of good judgment.

Answer for yourself *personally!* Eight to ten minutes should give you plenty of time.

1. Do you believe that people you know who have succeeded in business:

    a. are more clever than you?
    b. have good connections or money to start with?
    c. differ little from yourself but perhaps do work a little harder?

2. In school, were you more likely to choose courses emphasizing:

    a. research papers?
    b. lab work?
    c. examinations?

3. If you had an evening with little to do, would you most likely:

    a. visit a friend?
    b. work on a hobby?
    c. watch a TV program?

4. To get some exercise, would you prefer:

    a. running or road work at your own pace?
    b. joining a racquetball or tennis club?
    c. joining a neighborhood basketball or hockey team?

5. Which game would you rather play:

    a. Duplicate bridge?
    b. Black Jack?
    c. Monopoly?

6. When working with other folks on a committee, which of these would you look forward to with most pleasure:

   a. cooperating with others for the good of the project?
   b. convincing·other people to do what you want?
   c. other people coming up with good ideas?

7. In buying a major appliance, would you:

   a. talk with your friends, see what they bought and act accordingly?
   b. tend to buy an established, well-known brand, superior in performance?
   c. compare thoroughly the advantages of different brands?

8. In your daydreams, would you be most likely to appear as:

   a. a politician giving an election night victory speech?
   b. a private detective who is pondering a baffling case?
   c. a millionaire living in a villa at St. Tropez?

9. Your boss asks you to take over a company project that is failing. Would you say that you will:

   a. give an answer after you look into it further?
   b. take it?
   c. won't because you're too busy with other things?

10. While on a business trip in Europe you find you will be late for an appointment due to an indefinite delay in the train. Would you:

    a. reschedule your appointment?
    b. wait for the next train?
    c. rent a car?

11. Do you view yourself as:

    a. very popular—well liked—interested in people?
    b. superior—tough minded—not universally popular?
    c. loyal—hard-working—work well with others?

12. You operate an office cleaning service. A good friend and competitor dies suddenly. Would you:

    a. propose a merger to his wife?
    b. offer his customers a better deal?
    c. reassure his wife that you will never try to take away any customers?

13. An employee who is also a personal friend is not doing his job well. Do you:

    a. give him a warning and fire him if he doesn't change?
    b. leave him alone and hope he shapes up?
    c. hint that things are not going right and hope he gets the message?

14. Do you enjoy playing cards most when you:

    a. play with people who challenge you?
    b. play with good friends?
    c. play for high stakes?

15. You come home to spend a relaxing evening and find that your toilet has overflowed. Would you:

    a. call a plumber?
    b. call a handy friend to fix it for you?
    c. try to fix it yourself?

Answers and explanations will be found on the next page.

Answers—Entrepreneurial Exam

1. c	9. a
2. a	10. c
3. b	11. b
4. a	12. b
5. a	13. a
6. c	14. a
7. c	15. c
8. b	

Score one point for each correct answer. Questions 2, 3, 4, 8, 10 and 15 illustrate whether you are a realistic problem solver who can run a business without constant help from others.

Questions 5, 7 and 9 probe whether you take calculated risks and seek information before you act.

Questions 1, 6, 12 and 14 show whether you, like the classic entrepreneur, find other people most satisfying when they help fulfill your need to win.

Question 13 reveals whether you take responsibility for your destiny—and your business.

Question 11 gives us your opinion of self-worth—an essential ingredient.

If you score between 11 and 14 points, you could have a good chance to succeed. If you score from 7 to 10 points, you'd better have a superb business idea or a lot of money to help you out. If you score 7 or less, stay where you are.

If you scored 15, you peeked!

Small Businesses by Category Most Likely to Succeed . . . or Fail

I constantly revise and re-evaluate the business prospects within category. This is most difficult because of regional and seasonal variables. And of course, we must face the fact that most small businesses are in some measure the cult of the owner's personality. The clever entrepreneur in a business listed in the "worst" category has a much better chance of success than an incompetent, regardless of how promising his "best" business category appears.

Among the current best:

1. Building Material and Supply Stores—Increased do-it-yourself activity should boost sales up to 15% this current year. Residential construction and alteration looks strong.
2. Sports and Recreation Clubs— Racquetball Court Clubs are booming. Tennis centers are stabilizing after phenomenal growth. An increased awareness in the benefit of exercise is

the key. Clubs require large investments, but banks like them and profits are good.

3. Liquor Stores—Industry growth at retail level is excellent, possibly 12% in the current year. A creative businessman can expect high profits on each dollar of sales. Liquor retailing is not available in some states.

4. Foundries and Stove Manufacturers— OSHA tried hard to ruin the entire industry. Now those foundries remaining are getting excellent mark ups. The stove business is going to be booming for many years yet—watch this and all energy-related fields closely—opportunities abound!

5. Automobile Dealerships, Fuel Oil and Beer Distributors—With the right circumstances of location, brand and acquisition price, these can be great. They tend to move in families—ask your business broker!

6. Funeral Homes & Crematories—No fooling around here. These businesses are now making $9,200 to $11,500 on every $100,000 that they take in. Although the death rate continues its decline, the actual number of deaths will increase as the senior citizen population grows.

7. Auto Tire and Accessories Stores— Again it's the do-it-yourself trend that will help produce an annual growth rate in this type of business of nearly ten per cent this year.

8. Florist, Lawn and Garden Supply Centers—The profit ratios here are excellent and improving growth is running about nine per cent ahead of last year. Of interest in this area is federal funding now available for purchase of a center at low rates.

9. Office Supplies and Equipment—This has always been a consistent and steady leader in profit per dollar sales. A company with one million sales can return $50,000 with good future growth potential.

10. Hardware Stores—These also benefit from do-it-yourselfers and new merchandising methods that have doubled gross profits. High profits mean that you don't have to be a giant in the business in order to make a very nice living. A volume of $500,000 could easily return $30,000 to an entrepreneur owner/manager. You do not need a franchise in this field to be successful.

11. Engineering, Technical and Scientific Sales—Manufacturers in this area as well as distributors will profit from increased industry activity. Gross volume of sales in this business should increase 14% within the year.

12. Sporting Goods Manufacturers and Retailers—Wide ranging and increased participation in all forms of sporting activity is producing growth in all sports ranging from 8% to 60%. Some areas are leveling out this year; however, the

overview is excellent in this activity
area.

The worst:

1. Local Laundries and Dry Cleaners. Since 1972, improved home laundry systems and the increasing use of synthetic fabrics have slowed growth in this business. Older, established cleaners have stayed alive by providing extra services, such as rug cleaning.
2. Used-car Dealerships. Many banks have soured on making loans to used-car dealers because of the high risk involved. Current predictions show the business shrinking in the next few years. New car dealers are in the market with both feet.
3. Gas Stations. Competition and thinning profits have tarnished these once lucrative franchises. To earn $30,000 a year, a station would have to gross about 1.8 million.
4. Local Trucking Firms. The high cost of unionized labor and governmental regulation make this a risky enterprise. Growth prospects are sluggish at the present time.
5. Bakeries. Supermarket bakery departments make survival difficult for small independent stores. Shops that make it do so by offering specialized services.
6. Restaurants & Bars (easy entry businesses). No other business attracts as many prospective entrepreneurs as this one does. Growth potential is good,

about 10% in the next year, and profits aren't all that bad, about 3.5% *if you are successful.* Still, for every one that succeeds, probably a dozen fail for lack of management know-how. Fast-food franchises offer management assistance, but a major franchise like McDonald's or Burger King requires a cash investment of $85,000 or more.

7. Infants' Clothing Stores. Babies are not booming right now and retail clothing stores, particularly small independent ones, are running into considerable difficulty because of slow demand and stiff competition.
8. Machine Shops. Just too many in most areas. Over 5,000 independent shops make this business highly competitive. Each $100,000 in sales yields an average $3,300 in pretax profits.
9. Variety Stores, Small Neighborhood / Meat Stores. Unless these stores offer special services, like delivery, the going gets rough.
10. Car Washes. High turnover, strong competition and high capital investment make this one of the least attractive businesses for the entrepreneur.
11. Residential Construction Contractor. This business is slowly coming back, but banks are still wary and competition is stiff—financing and development problems further complicate things.

A Good Reference

1. An all important reference is the *Annual Statement Studies* published by Robert Morris Associates, 1432 PNB Building, Philadelphia, Pa. 19107.
The book is compiled of information gathered from American bankers and contains valuable information on the profitability of over 300 different types of business.
These facts are broken down as to the size and location of the endeavor.
The book sells for $13.95, but most libraries have it in the reference section, and you can be sure your local banker has a copy. He'll be happy to let you take a look.

2. Small Business Reporter, Department 3120, Bank of America, San Francisco, California 94120. $1.00 per copy. The "Business Operations" series is helpful for general information on running a business. Titles include: *Opening Your*

Own Business, Small Business Success, How to Buy or Sell A Business, Financing Small Business, Personnel for the Small Business, Steps to Starting A Business. Other series are "Business Profiles," which cover specific small businesses and "Professional Management" for doctors, dentists, veterinarians.

3. The SBA provides a series of pamphlets, leaflets and booklets which are either free or available for a very slight charge. Of particular interest are the: *Starting and Managing Series* and *Small Business Management Series.* These booklets contain a wealth of advice for prices ranging from $.20 to $.70.
Aids Annuals contain more information at prices up to $1.25 per volume. These include information for small businesses, small manufacturers, and small marketers. *Aids* for the current year are available at no cost.
Suggested Management Guides ($1.25), *Managing for Profits* ($.65), and *Buying and Selling A Small Business* are non-series publications that are excellent general information sources.
The SBA and *Small Business Reporter* series are the *best* sources for written materials which can help you do your job better. Many libraries will have copies of them.

4. *How to Organize and Operate a Small Business,* Clifford Baumback, Kenneth

Lawyer, and Pearce Kelley, 5th edition, Prentice-Hall, Inc., Englewood Cliffs, New Jersey, 1973. This book is an outstanding source of information and is used widely as a text. In addition to providing an in-depth overview of small business operation and policy, it includes an excellent topical bibliography. You will probably find this in your library.

5. *Business Resource Directory,* Urban Affairs Section, Federal Reserve Bank of Boston, 2nd edition, 1975. This 260-page handbook lists sources of free and low-cost technical assistance for New England businesspeople. Groups are arranged by state and city and are cross-indexed according to the type of services they provide. The publication is free and may be obtained by writing to Business Resource Directory, Urban Affairs, Federal Reserve Bank of Boston, 30 Pearl St., Boston, Mass. 02106.

*Freedom of enterpise is more
than the freedom to succeed . . .
at the core it is freedom to fail.
This country owes its greatness
to men who are free to take
chances and dare to do it!*

Ray Eppert
Burroughs Corp.

In Summary

I've often noticed the early winners tend to stay winners. Often their youthful wins are the small accomplishments of high school athletes, college scholastic success or achievement and recognition while working for others. Winning is something as basic as raising some fine kids. (No mean accomplishment, this!)

However, all the winners I know are different and possess unique and surprising qualities that are evident again and again. It's fine to fantasize about a higher income and better life; but to a few people it's more than an idle dream. They do something about it and they rise rapidly. Perhaps as you've read this book you've felt this is a practical possibility for you.

Let me warn you that some of the characteristics that you must cultivate *may not get you elected Miss Congeniality* (but then, do you really care?). Other people may have other life goals, but high on *your* list *must* be the drive to *achieve* in terms of money and business success.

To be an achiever, one evidently needs certain personality traits that other people sometimes find undesirable or even downright offensive! But if the idea of having greater wealth is appealing to you, you may determine that you want to be an achiever after all. (So welcome to the club!)

Successful achievers seem to be distinguished by five outstanding traits. Not every achiever displays every trait, of course, but these five characteristics are so common among these fast-rising men and women, and so much less common among non-achievers.

1. *Single-minded Pragmatism:* Studies of materially successful people turn up this trait again and again. I have analyzed the differences between fast and slow climbers in the business world, and there is a very large element of pragmatism in the personalities of fast-rising men and women. These people want great career success, aren't afraid to admit it and, to get it, will do things that other people simply won't do.

Slow-rising people often have a strong "moralistic orientation" instead of a pragmatic one. If asked what they value most in life they emphasize concepts like trust, loyalty and honor—or attitudes such as "self-fulfillment."

The achievers don't necessarily scorn those concepts, but they value other things just as highly or more highly: business success, leadership, status, and, many of them will admit it frankly, *money.*

If you fall into the group of folks who say "satisfaction from my work—one of the joys of my life" (and you really mean it) you've got this all important personality trait.

2. *Self Reliance:* It probably isn't surprising that the winners tend to be loners. Many of them simply don't like working closely with other people because, as one high-earning business consultant told me recently, "other people hold me back."

The loner psychology shows up just as clearly among achievers who earn corporate paychecks. "I think of myself as self-employed even though I work for a big company." "I even have a little dialogue I recite to keep myself on my toes." "Do I work for the company? No, for me. I'll never let myself forget it."

Company loyalty is not a big trait among "winners I have known." A fact that I have long observed is that the real winners have old number one in first place.

3. *Self-Testing:* One common misconception about successful small business-persons is that they are invariably high risk-takers, constantly flirting with financial disaster. This may be true of some self-employed entrepreneurs, but usually the opposite is the case.

Studies have shown people with a high need for achievement, in which category I include my winners, characteristically do take risks; but these risks are frequently hedged to limit the risk-taker's loss.

I often find the successful entrepreneurs full of enthusiasm, working like hell in a job which is really just a little too big for their talents. Once they get things under control, the job ceases to be challenging and they're off to match themselves against another tough challenge.

They don't usually take huge financial risks that would damage their careers or put them "down the tube." They simply relish going the full fifteen rounds with the top contenders.

In contrast, the "slow riser" wants to be comfortable. He's the kind of guy that arranges tennis matches only with those he can beat quite easily. The slow riser certainly does not want to risk testing his physical prowess, intelligence, talent and judgment in order to succeed. Words like "tenure" and "job security" have a comforting ring for the slow riser.

4. *Think for Yourself:* For decades, psychologists have been using an artful and rather unkind test to determine how easily a person can be swayed by other people's judgments. Half a dozen people gather around a table on which lie three items, one a bit shorter in length than the other two. They are all asked to say whether they think the items are all the same length; however only one person is actually being tested. Unknown to him or her, all the others are "ringers" who have been instructed in advance to say that the items are all the same length.

The person being tested sometimes trusts what his or her own eyes see and insists that one item is shorter. More often, however, he gets overwhelmed by the majority opinion and will agree that they're the same length.

In one study, the results showed that those whose incomes were unusually high were unlikely to let their independent judgment be influenced in this way. Instead, they stuck with what their own senses told them. In fact, some just saw through the whole experiment. They simply will not go along with the herd.

5. *A Sense of Self Worth is Important:* Winners, as a breed, seem perfectly sure they are superior to others in the qualities they consider important: intellect, toughness, staying power. Many winners are highly arrogant, which is yet another reason they aren't universally popular.

But this feeling of superiority helps them immeasurably in the long climb. For one thing, it helps them make decisions quickly, cleanly and forcefully, and commit themselves strongly to each decision once it is made.

A sense of your own self worth is important. I really don't believe you can succeed without it. . .

My Parting Shot

Take care of yourself . . .
Good health is your major source of
wealth . . .
Without it, happiness is nearly impossible.

Be intensively physical and active—Savor
life with gusto and vigor . . .

Keep your life plan simple/rural/basic . . .
Keep your goals within reach—Use strategy
to reach goals, not objectives.

Always be of good cheer. If your friend loses
his smile, lend him yours.

Avoid the angry, dull, abrasive, intense
persons. The tensions of their crusades
render them humorless and a boring waste
of your time.

Give advice only when it benefits you . . .
Never give free advice . . . Wise men don't
want it . . . And fools won't heed it.

Be tender and loyal in love . . . It's (by far) the most enriching life force we have . . . Be compassionate of the sick and aged . . . tolerant of the poor, stupid, weak, and wrong . . .

Never forget that the dreams and plans of any acquisition always bring more delight than the ultimate material possession.

Lastly . . . Consistently enrich your mind . . .Read, study, travel. Resolve to listen more, talk less . . . Never stop learning, striving to improve your awareness and sharpening your winning game.

. . . For you must have realized by now that . . . All moments of happiness are serendipitous and cannot of themselves be pursued. . . . They rush in beautiful torrents where life is seized with zest and purpose.

Remember Lin U Tang—"The purpose of living may be simply for the enjoyment of it."

So embrace life and its opportunities. . .

Mind your own business. . .

And. . .

May your endeavors prosper.

Index